1 7 8 9

The Emblems of Reason

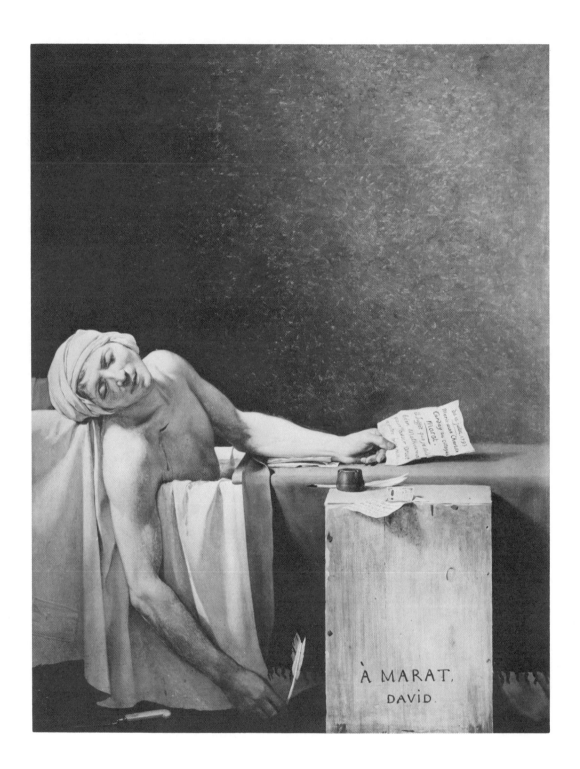

1 7 8 9

The Emblems of Reason

JEAN STAROBINSKI

Translated by Barbara Bray

University Press of Virginia

Charlottesville

FRONTISPIECE: *Jacques-Louis David (1748–1825).* Death of Marat. 1793.
(Brussels, Musées royaux des Beaux-Arts de Belgique.
Photo Giraudon)

FIRST PUBLISHED *1982*

Originally published in 1973 as
1789: Les Emblèmes de la Raison *by Jean Starobinski*

© 1973, Istituto Editoriale Italiano, Milano
© 1979, Flammarion, Paris, pour l'édition française
The notes to the present edition have been expanded by the author.

Library of Congress Cataloging in Publication Data

Starobinski, Jean.
  1789, the emblems of reason.

  Translation of: 1789, les emblèmes de la raison.
  Bibliography: p.
  Includes index.
  1. Neoclassicism (Art) 2. Arts and revolutions.
3. France—History—Revolution, 1789—Influence.
I. Title. II. Title: Seventeen eighty-nine, the emblems of reason.
NX452.5.N4S7   709'44.   81–13135   ISBN 0–8139–0915–5   AACR2

PRINTED IN THE UNITED STATES OF AMERICA

Contents

1 7 8 9

The Emblems of Reason

1 7 8 9

T HE YEAR 1789 is a watershed in the political history of Europe. Is it also a turning point in the evolution of style? At first sight it does not seem to have produced any major event or significant development in the history of art. The "return to antiquity" preceded the Revolution: Neoclassicism started to take hold from about the middle of the eighteenth century, and the forms it adopted under the Revolution were invented before 1789. What the Revolution can be credited with is its fervent stress on the Roman and republican rather than the Alexandrian elements in neoclassicism; its widespread dissemination of imagery through propaganda and counterpropaganda; and its introduction of public ceremonial. This may seem a disappointing result, especially as there is a negative side to the balance: The crisis years of the Revolution reduced to almost complete inactivity such artists as depended on the patronage of the aristocracy and the wealthy. Architects, portrait painters, cabinetmakers, and jewelers fell on hard times. Many of those who, like Louis David, supported the Revolution became its official artists; many others were forced to make ends meet by practicing such minor arts as illustration and engraving. Some who had close connections with the nobility emigrated as early as 1789; and they were not soon replaced. Art is probably better at expressing states of civilization than moments of violent change. More recent examples have shown that revolutions do not immediately discover an artistic language corresponding to the new political order. Inher-

[5]

1) HUBERT ROBERT (1733–1808).
The Bastille during the First Days of Its Demolition. 1789.

(Paris, Musée Carnavelet. Photo Bulloz)

ited forms continued to be used even though people want to proclaim the old world a thing of the past.

If we look at 1789 we see the advent of the Revolution, but not its long-term effects. We can try to understand its emergence when it was still close to its immediate causes, to its portents and premonitory symptoms. But most of the works of art that came into being in 1789 are not to be regarded as products of the Revolution. Buildings, paintings, operas, and so on were completed both in France and elsewhere at the time when the mob threatened Paris and the French monarchy was toppling. Such creations, begun beforehand and based on a sustained intention that owed nothing to the fever of those ardent days, need to be interpreted independent of their immediate historical context, for they are not related to it in terms of simple cause and effect.

But the fact that they coincided with the Revolution is not without significance. Like them, the Revolution derived from earlier ideas and a previous moral climate that it now brought into the open. The history of the year 1789, the violent consecration of a social transformation which had been long preparing and was already partly accomplished, consisted of a series of spectacular events linked together like the scenes in a tragedy and luridly lit.[1] More than at any other time in history it is as if we were looking at a written text with a style of its own. Even at the time some commentators saw 1789 as a page written by the hand of God or of the people.[2] So it is legitimate, and even necessary, to compare the style of the Revolution as an event with the style of the works of art produced in the same period. In the absence of any direct causal connection, let us examine the message which seemed to arise out of the contemporary situation. Art and history throw light on and give clues about one another, even when they conflict rather than corroborate.

In this comparison between works of art and events, events predominate. So vivid is the light given off by the Revolution that it illuminates every contemporary phenomenon. And the artists of 1789, whether they were concerned with it or ignored it, whether they approved of it or disapproved, were contemporaries of the Revolution. They cannot avoid being placed in relation to it: In a way, it is by it that they are judged. The Revolution imposes a universal criterion, distinguishing what is modern from what is obsolete. It introduces and applies a new norm of social relationship, a norm that works of art are forced either to accept or to reject.

THE

FREEZE

2) FRANCISCO DE GOYA (1746–1828). *Winter*. 1787.
(Madrid, Museo del Prado. Photo Anderson-Giraudon)

T HE WINTER of 1788–1789 was extremely cold. In Venice the lagoon froze over and people could walk across it. Some paintings of the scene survive, and everywhere engravings were made recording this memorable whim of the weather. There were ice floes in the Seine in Paris, and Hubert Robert, who liked to paint the capital in its various metamorphoses, made this unusual event the subject of a picture shown in the 1789 Salon.[1] France had had a poor harvest the previous summer, and the people were suffering, anxious, and restless. In the provinces there were riots and looting.

Goya, in a tapestry cartoon probably dating from before 1788, gives us the best idea of what such a winter could mean (fig. 2). Some pitiless force is at work in that icy, windswept darkness. Mere survival is a difficult task. Yet there are the peasants confronting the frost and going on their way. Some goal draws them on. The traveler braves the gusts of snow and tries to warm himself from within. One man huddles against another. A touching communion unites everything bent on survival.

Spring was late that year. In his *Voeux d'un solitaire* (Aspirations of a Recluse), Bernardin de Saint-Pierre relates:

On May 1 of this year 1789 I went down at sunrise into my garden to see how it was faring after the terrible winter, when the thermometer went down to 19 degrees below freezing on December 31. On the way I thought about the disas-

trous hailstorm which swept through the whole country on
July 13. When I entered the garden I found neither cabbages
nor artichokes nor white jasmine nor narcissi; almost all my
carnations and hyacinths had perished; my fig trees were dead,
and so were my laurustines, which usually flowered in January. As for my young ivy plants, most of them had withered
branches and rust-colored leaves.

But the rest of my plants were in good health, though
over three weeks late in their growth. My borders of strawberry plants, violets, thyme, and primulas were all dappled
with green and white and blue and crimson; and my hedges
of honeysuckle, raspberry, gooseberry, rose and lilac bushes
were covered with leaves and flower buds. Also in bloom were
my alleys of vines, apple trees, pears, peaches, cherries, and
apricots. To tell the truth, the buds of the vines were only just
starting to open; but the flowers on the apricot trees were
already fertilized.[2]

This closely observed plant world presented a dual
spectacle of life and death together. Its owner offers us
a rare magnification of the fleeting beauty of a garden
being born again out of its own destruction. Reading
his words, we seem to be outside history for a moment,
in a tiny world set apart from human events. Life and
death no longer have the same meaning as they do in
struggles between conflicting wills: Here they are only
natural phenomena, in harmony with the eternal order
of nature. We are tempted to think of the vegetable
kingdom as a refuge for a contemplative spirit dis-
mayed by the violence of history.[3]

Not so. For Bernardin de Saint-Pierre, the shadow
of history is clearly to be seen in the upheavals of nature. The text quoted above goes on to suggest that

hail, storm, and frost are much more than natural disasters: They are tangible images conveying in terms
of the physical universe incipient national bankruptcy,
the decay of institutions, and the sufferings of the
people. Natural disaster symbolizes the misfortunes of
the State: It is not their adventitious setting but their
visible manifestation. Conversely, spring with its upsurge of life offers an incentive to hope: It is a prophecy
of universal renewal.

People will say that such symbolic interpretation of
signs in the weather is typical of a naive (or more
probably falsely naive) mentality, ignorant of the
anonymous order of natural laws and claiming to read
Providential intention in a sphere that is really governed only by the concatenation of mechanical causes.[4]
What more anachronistic than such an attitude, derived
from the Bible and the scriptures, at a time when no
enlightened person still deigned to give them cre-
dence? Had not Bayle, Fontenelle, and Voltaire marked
"paid" to belief in signs and oracles?

And yet Bernardin de Saint-Pierre's reading of
things, which linked hail and frost to the disastrous
management of public finances, allows us to glimpse
an essential aspect of the attitude prevailing in the
spring of 1789. Financial disaster and meteorological
upheaval were two different facets in the same adver-
sity. The threat of national bankruptcy found cosmic
expression in the hailstorms of July 13, 1788; the in-
human blindness of the elements was reinforced and
reflected in the ineluctability of the deficit. The same
dark, unreasoning, hostile power was manifest in both.
The same obscure malevolence inhabited the heavens,

institutions, and the administration. The feudal system had taken on the harsh solidity of an actual instrument of oppression; the prodigality of princes and other great men deaf to all warnings had come to appear like some natural affliction.

The freeze. And the deficit.[5] Jean-Paul Rabaut Saint-Etienne, a Calvinist politician and pastor later guillotined, wrote: "It is impossible to describe the country's surprise . . . and indignation when it learned how enormous the deficit was: Up till then France's woes had been felt, but they had not yet been calculated." For members of the Third Estate the deficit was a cold numerical translation of the carousings and ceremonies of the court and the nobility. It was a frozen fete, the winter of the aristocratic grasshoppers who had spent the summer singing and dancing. The inconsistencies of the regime had been denounced by Beaumarchais's Figaro: "What it needed was a calculator; what it got was a dancer."[6] Now the minuet was over and the gamesters could no longer fling their money away: It was time for the settling of accounts.

Admittedly, expenditure on entertainment was not the only thing that had depleted the Treasury. Aid to the "insurgents" in America had also cost a pretty penny. But before people's very eyes there were the châteaus bought or built for the queen, and all the finery and fireworks and other wild extravagances. The account drawn up by the calculators was an indictment of a way of life that had reached its height in rococo and descended into more sobriety in Louis XVI. This style had been the embodiment of lavishness at every level of existence, whether material, emotional, or intellectual.

It had mixed and multiplied ornament and glittered from crystal, metal, and lacquer in a dazzle of ever-renewed brilliance. It was an art that had built around the rich and powerful a setting of perpetual festivity in which pleasure, wonder, and surprise only flagged in order to be born again after a brief eclipse. The rococo sensibility could include, between the bright gleams of agreeable moments, a temporary cloud and passing states of emptiness and exhaustion; but it put its trust in a capacity for renewal that roused the soul to new sensations, new and living ideas, new and stimulating images. In the same way the princes, after ruining themselves gambling, fell back on the generosity of the king, or on borrowing, or on their lands, which could provide them with fresh resources by means of direct income, taxes, or mortgages.

The luxury and ostentation of the clothes worn by the nobility and the clergy in the procession of the States General scandalized the ordinary people in that springtime of scarcity. These men of privilege without personal distinction, these "obscure eminences," as Madame de Staël called them, seemed to be usurping the honors they flaunted.[7] Rabaut Saint-Etienne, a representative of the Third Estate, described the scene:

> The senior clergy, glittering with gold, and all the great men of the kingdom, crowding around the dais, displayed the utmost magnificence, while the representatives of the Third Estate looked as if they were dressed in mourning. Yet their long line represented the nation, and the people were so conscious of this that they overwhelmed them with applause. They shouted "Long live the Third Estate!" just as they have since shouted "Long live the nation!" The unwise distinction

had produced the opposite effect to that intended by the court: The Third Estate recognized their fathers and defenders in the men in black coats and high cravats, and their enemies in the others. . . . These men, who had never before traveled beyond their own provinces, and who had left behind them the sight of destitution in town and country, now saw evidence of the extravagant expenditure of Louis XIV and Louis XV, and of the new court's quest for pleasure. This château here, they were told, cost two hundred million; the fairy palace at Saint-Cloud cost twelve; and no one knows how much has been spent on the Petit Trianon. And they answered, "All this magnificence was produced by the sweat of the people."[8]

It was a crucial moment. For those onlookers who had learned to count, the magic of pomp and circumstance no longer worked. Mere expense no longer inspired wonder and respect; what mattered was the labor out of which these palaces were built. The humble people without whom brilliant society would never have enjoyed its decor of illusion were about to make their grievances heard.

For those who condemned it and wanted to do away with it, the world now coming to an end took on the aspect of evil itself. It was the expression of an active determination to reject universal good, shutting itself up foolishly in its own pleasures and so becoming the equivalent of a natural accident, an affliction that sensible people must fight and bring under control.

But let us enter for a few moments the world of the aristocrats in 1789 and try to see it from within, as it saw itself. What we find is a secret complicity with the condemnation that was falling upon that world from without. Even in its most outrageous pleasures it was haunted by a sense of death and fascinated with the idea of surcease. It had nothing with which to oppose its enemies; it gave in. It had an uneasy conscience. It had listened to its accusers, such as Rousseau and Beaumarchais, and it had dreamed of reforms and philanthropy and regeneration. But it had not thrown off the habit of indulging in expensive amusements; so it ran headlong to its ruin. A certain number of works of art and literature, keen, cynical, and intelligent, reflected the feeling that something was coming to an end; sometimes this art, linked to a class that was on the way out, exhibits not only signs of exhaustion but also an admirable freedom, the result of the breaking of all ties and of the intoxication felt by those about to die because they have nothing more to lose.[9] The paradox is that such works of extravagance and caprice, products of a moribund society, occasionally, in their boldness and marvelous ease, show an inventiveness and creative audacity that we seek for in vain in works where the artist sets out to serve, practically and morally, a new social and political order.

VENICE

AT

SUNSET

3) FRANCESCO GUARDI (1712–1793). *The Gray Lagoon.*
    (Milan, Museo Poldi-Pezzoli)

T IME WAS running out for the aristocratic republic of Venice. The art of Guardi, who was to die at the age of eighty on January 1, 1793, was shedding its last rays. A whole aspect of rococo died with him. His son Giacomo would never be anything but a decent popularizer, anxious to see his father's "errors" forgiven. But what a glorious end Guardi's was, and how it foretold the painting of the future! *The Gray Lagoon* and *The Fire at San Marcuola* (1789) are closer to us than neoclassical art: They are a magnificent anticipation of the spirit of impressionism, and, over and above impressionism, of one of the most fundamental functions of painting, which is to glorify space and light (figs. 3, 4). In these canvases and drawings, light reigns alone, transient but above the even more transient agitation of men: For the passing state of the light and the passing moment of the day take on an aspect of the absolute. In the *Fire*, the crowd seems to be part of the conflagration: The human figures are somber sparks flying from the blaze. The glow of disaster acts as a unifying principle.

It was perhaps to depict Gianantonio Selva's neoclassical facade of La Fenice (completed in 1792) that Guardi took up his pen and brushes for the last time, to set down figures that appear and disappear in the twinkling of an eye (fig. 5). The drawing captures the wide expanse of sky, the part of it swept by clouds, their scattered shadows, the mysterious swirling of the air, and the precise but faintly trembling architecture. The ephemeral passer-by—a little blur, literally trans-

[23]

4) FRANCESCO GUARDI (1712–1793). *The Fire at San Marcuola.* 1789. (Venice, Museo Correr. Photo Toso)

lating the Italian technical term *macchietta*—is no more than an accident of the light. Man fades into the city he has created, and the city fades into the space in which it lives and breathes.

There is a fairylike, gossamer quality about the last works in which Guardi set down worldly festivities, the series of drawings recording the marriage of the

[24]

5) FRANCESCO GUARDI (1712–1793). *La Fenice*. 1792.
(Venice, Museo Correr. Photo Toso)

son of the duke of Polignac (1790). The chairs in the
drawing of the banquet have an ironic, graceful life of
their own: Spaced out with flawless regularity, they
unconsciously symbolize the lordly puerility of the aristocratic etiquette that separates those it brings together
(fig. 6). In the drawing of the nuptial blessing the
movement of the crowd is a continuation of the sinuous

[25]

6 + 7)   FRANCESCO GUARDI (1712–1793).
*Wedding Ceremonies of the duke of
Polignac at Carpenedo.* 1790.
(Venice, Museo Correr. Photo Toso)

lines of the rococo church: Men themselves are only part of the general decor, obeying an invisible stage director who stamps the whole spectacle with the whim of arabesque, within which there are minor waves and undulations as there may be mordents, appoggiaturas, and gruppetti in a melody (figs. 7, 8). But Guardi's art contains no sarcasm: The extreme lightness of touch and general airiness seem to reflect an aloof smile and the contemplative wisdom that could tune the swift passage of the pencil to the swift passage of time.

THE END OF VENICE found its legendary historian—its mythographer—in Giandomenico Tiepolo. His drawings and frescoes show the almost limitless freedom of an art that confronts its own death; a strange combination of decline and frenzy.

Having collaborated with his father, he was well acquainted with the secrets of painting great allegorical murals and had no rival at creating an imaginary but convincing horizon on the walls of a reception room. In his work aerial perspectives are no longer those of the great baroque tradition, in which the sky opened on to an ecstasy of eternity. The depths of the zenith are no longer inhabited by the glory of God. Eternity has vanished. What is left are torn clouds, a sky swept by earthly winds, and a forest landscape strewn by capricious nature with rugged details—lowering rocks, twisted trees, a bleak violence, and the weird and inexhaustible comedy of the animal kingdom. Giandomenico rejected prettification and easy grace: His harsh idylls feature poverty-stricken peasants, pigs, and half-

8) FRANCESCO GUARDI (1712–1793).
Wedding Ceremonies of the duke of Polignac at Carpenedo. 1790.
(Venice, Museo Correr. Photo Toso)

starved curs. This nature is not the refuge of sensitive
souls. It is full of creatures that are fierce, grotesque, or
macabre. Giandomenico Tiepolo delighted in drawing
skeletons and moths (fig. 9). To inhabit and rule his
disturbing universe, he resurrected the violent shapes
of mythology: The lord of creation is not man but the

centaur or the satyr, hairy, sinewy, and swift. But this
asperity is still compatible with playful elegance and
rueful laughter. For everything is a subject for laughter.
When Giandomenico transcribes the familiar scenes of
Venetian life he always ends up in sarcasm and caricature. He always brings in some kind of unreality, some
supple yet wan fantasy. Longhi seems timid in comparison. At one moment acrobats whose virtuosity
makes them seem boneless perform before misshapen
spectators. At another, potbellied or humpbacked landowners, grimacing foolishly, ape the rituals of distinguished society. But this world is haunted by one
omnipresent and obsessional figure: Pulcinella (in English, Punchinello or Punch), a character who has es-
caped from the theater to mingle in everyday life and
tinge it with his own unreality and mockery. He is to
be found everywhere. In the arms of the centaur who
carries him off. Eating with the satyr in his lair. One of
the mountebanks' audience. A nonchalant companion
of patricians as they go for a stroll. Amid all the faces
that are really masks, he deliberately wears his own
black mask with its hooked nose. We do not know
whether his hump or his paunch are real or false. His
enormous white hat is always on his head and seems to
be part of him. Pulcinella proliferates: He is not so
much a single character as a horde of offshoots. Giandomenico seems to have had a sort of comic nightmare
in which this troop of invaders, for whom life consists
of absurd revels, endeavored to drive all the rest of
mankind out of Venice. Giandomenico, more cruel
than Carlo Gozzi, who had tried to revive the dying
commedia del arte, intermingles a senile world with

9) GIANDOMENICO TIEPOLO (1727–1804). *Moths.*
(Udine, Civici Musei e Gallerie di Storia ed Arte.
Photo Brisighelli)

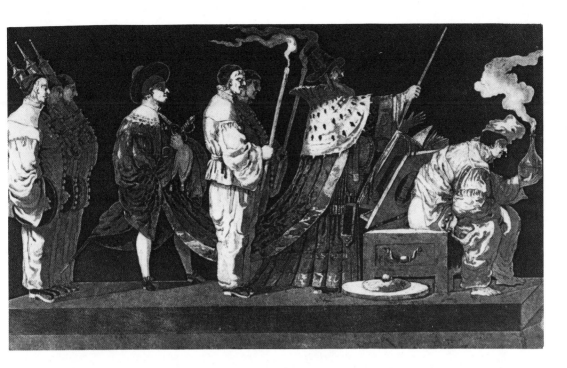

10) LOUIS-JEAN DESPREZ (1743–1804).
The Great Doctor Pantaloon Explaining Medical Science. 1790.
(Stockholm, Kungliga Biblioteket)

figures of childhood, as if to show that Pulcinella's in-
fantile idleness is the fundamental truth of a society
whose historical role is outgrown. It is as if some sudden mutation had produced a little Pulcinella in every
family, to spend the rest of his life not in work and other
productive occupations but just performing empty gestures at an eternal party. This figure, omnipresent
among characters from mythology and the survivors of
patrician families, may be seen as the symbol of a confusion undermining all hierarchies and traditional distinctions. Pulcinella is the active agent of a joyful return
to chaos. For the people in Giandomenico's world, *il
mondo nuovo* is an illusion. There is not going to be a
new world. The spectacle they gather round to see

[31]

11)   LOUIS-JEAN DESPREZ (1743–1804). *Enema.* 1790.
(Stockholm, Kungliga Biblioteket)

consists of misleading images; the common people
yield to the fascination of this lowly stage. But Pulcinella is mortal. His tricks, harbingers of the end of a
world, themselves have an end. Giandomenico even-
tually depicted him on his deathbed, dropsical from
drinking too much wine, a Silenus who has lost all the
grace of Dionysus while retaining his cap and mask to
the last. A doctor with ass's ears, cousin to the Great
Doctor derided by Desprez, observes that his pulse has
stopped (figs. 10, 11).[1]

MOZART

BY

NIGHT

I T WAS the Venice of Giandomenico Tiepolo that brought forth Mozart's librettist Lorenzo da Ponte. This versifying adventurer did not create anything new—the masterpieces were Mozart's—but he had remarkable intuitions. We should not be too ready to look down on the libretto of *Così fan tutte* (1790). In it, flattering masks and ready-made protestations triumph over a love that thought itself eternal. The Albanians have only to appear, all bedizened, offering a mere caricature of love, and the deceitful present overcomes the memory of tearful vows and farewells. In the naively faithless hearts of Fiordiligi and Dorabella, love is as the age of rococo saw it—an agitation linked to the magic of the fleeting moment, a dizzy attraction without a future or a past. The favored lover is always he who is clever enough to be there. And it is this cruel truth which, through Mozart's divining genius, throws a veil of melancholy over this apparently playful work. At the wedding feast, after the *marche militaire* which heralds the return of the past, the fiancés meet again and forgive one another in a setting designed to celebrate the apotheosis of inconstancy. Forgiveness makes all else forgotten. Love has conquered. But it triumphs over its own ruins, in a twilight where each young man is reunited with a mistress who had decked herself out for another. In this scene I like to see the young brides dressed in the exaggerated fashions of the day, in loose peignoirs or high-waisted gowns *à l'anglaise*, emphasizing the curve of the hips; with a wisp of muslin around the very low necks, tall coiffures with ringlets in the nape of the neck, and jewelery echoing the sparkle of goblets and chandeliers.

The Marriage of Figaro (1786) had already given Mozart a chance to bring an opera to a close in a marvelous nocturne of agitation, disillusion, and tenderness. The music lends the plot a dimension probably undreamed of by Beaumarchais, imaging the confusion and disorder that blur social differences and mingle bitterness and pleasure, disguise and illusion, sin and forgiveness. After a wild day's pursuit of love among the pines of a great park, order is restored to rank and feeling only through a redoubling of disorder and deceit. For a moment we have been on the brink of chaos and madness.[1]

In *Don Giovanni* (1787), many of the scenes take place at night: the murder, the ball, the scene in the graveyard. And the ultimate darkness falls on the libertine's supper and the fateful arrival of the guest of stone. On the eve of happenings that were to mark the end of an age, the confrontation between the seducer and the *uom di sasso* takes on a further meaning in addition to the traditional implications of the legend. Don Juan is a man of prodigality and excess, of fleeting moments and short-lived conquests. He lives without counting: It is his servant who calculates and keeps the record, the ledger of the *mill' e tre*. For Don Juan the measure is never full; bounds exist only to be broken; his only religion is liberty. Liberty authorizes this "erotic ogre," as Pierre Jean Jouve has called him, to make his life a continual feast.[2] In the first instance the freedom Don Juan lays claim to is no more than an affirmation of the limitlessness of sensual enjoyment. The same frenzy is to be seen in Sade: Despite the apparent definiteness of the figure in the title of *The 120 Days*, it really symbolizes boundlessness. But this freedom is not unconnected with the feeling that later inspired the men of the Revolution. It has been rightly observed that when Don Juan exclaims *"Viva la libertà!"* the libertine and freethinker takes on the aspect of a "libertarian." The passion for limitlessness, which refuses to recognize the restraints of religion, is also unable to accept the compartments and barriers of a strict social order, and in order to break them down the *"libertin"* appeals to reason and uses moral arguments. Its own logic makes the passion for limitlessness unwilling to restrict itself to governing the life of a privileged individual; it aims at becoming universal, at extending to the whole human race. This tendency is constantly evident in Sade. Baudelaire put his finger on the truth when he wrote that the Revolution was the work of voluptuaries, by which he meant the men whose every inclination linked them to the world that was dying and who, though they turned against it and became its sworn enemies, were faithful witnesses to its disorder, its free speculation, and its contradictory appetites. They were still dominated by that society's obsession with death at the very moment when they were dealing it incurable wounds. They were men of the Ancien Régime, and when they gave that regime the coup de grace they were only bringing to fruition the seeds of doom that lay within it. They thus emerge as the first soldiers in the revolutionary camp, but warriors who were later overtaken by the Revolution and buried beneath other waves. The heroic yet scandalous figure of Mirabeau is typical here.

Don Giovanni bows to his legendary fate. He defiantly proffers his hand to the statue, the thunderbolt strikes, and the earth swallows him up. Victory goes to the old order, the outraged father, ultimate revenge. But this ethos, which formed part of a long baroque tradition, was not alien to the prerevolutionary mentality. It contrasted unstable desire, discontinuity, and the episodic moments of debauchery with the cold eternity of the statue, which represented good faith, inflexible justice, and a permanent divine order immune to outrage. At a time when the privileged classes were increasingly drawn toward extravagance and immorality, it was inevitable that, in the minds of the very people who were being sucked into the whirlpool, the figure they so obstinately denied should loom larger: the figure that stood for the permanent, the immutable, the transcendent. In the Don Juan myth the style of baroque living is exhibited in its utmost degree, and at the same time subjected to out-and-out condemnation. On the eve of the crisis in which the world of baroque (and of its substitute, rococo) was to disappear, it was more or less necessary for that condemnation to be repeated and for bad conscience to be able to inflict imaginary expiation on itself by damning Valmont and Don Juan. The men of 1787 were probably in a better position to see the striking down of Don Juan as the last and supreme moment in a life made up entirely of fleeting moments. They knew from their own experience that desire, with its endless quest for pleasure, yearns broodingly to end, to find rest, to soothe the weariness of time with death. By the time freedom in debauchery had reached this point, a darker background could be seen through the brilliance of enjoyment and festivity. But when retribution strikes the "*libertin*," whose is the triumph? Does it belong to the God of traditional theology? To the morality of a regenerate society? Or does it rather belong to the mortal power lurking in the depths of pleasure?

As far as Mozart's last opera is concerned there is no doubt about it. In *The Magic Flute* (1791) the victorious power is divine; but it belongs to a divinity greatly modified by contemporary deism. The dawn that breaks at the end and drives away Monostatos and the Queen of the Night is solar Good: "*Die Strahlen der Sonne vertreiben die Nacht.*"

Daybreak celebrates the union of beauty and virtue: Pamina, daughter of the Queen of the Night, will belong to Prince Tamino, whose love has survived unfailingly, in silence and solitude, a long series of tests. Much has been said about the weakness and naiveté of Schikaneder's libretto and about his indebtedness to Gozzi, Wieland, and the Abbé Terrasson. But he kept to the great and simple images of the esoteric. He retained the fervor of freemasonry, which erected benevolence into a cosmic principle. (Mozart, like many of his contemporaries, belonged to a Masonic lodge and wrote music for Masonic ceremonies. The last work he conducted, in 1791, was a cantata on friendship.)[3] It is absolutely basic to *The Magic Flute* that all should end in a new age, a glorious beginning, a reconciliation restoring unity: The purified hero takes as his bride one who is heiress both to the world of day and to the frenzy of night, for Pamina is daughter at once of a beneficient magician and of the dark queen. Out of this allegorical synthesis, Mozart's music creates a great ceremony of mystery and joy.[4]

THE

SOLAR MYTH

OF THE

REVOLUTION

METAPHORS OF light triumphing over darkness, life being reborn out of death, and the world being brought back to its beginning were to be found everywhere in the period leading up to 1789. For these simple similes and ageless antitheses, charged from time immemorial with religious values, that age seemed to have a special and passionate predilection.[1] Once the old order had been symbolically reduced to the semblance of a dark cloud or cosmic scourge, the struggle against it could, by the same process, represent its object as the advent of light. Once the self-evidence of reason and feeling took on the force of a law of light, any relationship of authority or obedience that was not based upon it was bound to belong to darkness. The same Apollonian image is to be found repeated over and over again in writings of 1789, in connection with all kinds of subjects (fig. 12). "All the hopes of the nation then turned toward M. Necker, just as people look for the rays of the sun after a long and disastrous storm."[2] The poets used endless variations of the same image in hymning the taking of the Bastille. Alfieri, Klopstock, and Blake all saw themselves as witnesses of a great dawn:

But the dens shook and trembled, the prisoners look up and
  assay to shout; they listen,
Then laugh in the dismal den, then are silent, and a light walks
  round the dark towers.
For the Commons convene in the Hall of the Nation; like spirits
  of fire in the beautiful

[43]

Porches of the Sun, to plant beauty in the desert craving abyss,
    they gleam
On the anxious city; all children new-born first behold them;
    tears are fled,
And they nestle in earth-breathing bosoms.

                [Blake, *The French Revolution*, 1791][3]

This mythical projection, so far removed from the strict truth of what actually happened, gives some idea of how the event struck people's imagination, with effects spreading far beyond just Paris and France. The French themselves believed that in overthrowing abuse and privilege, in destroying the great citadel of despotism that had overshadowed Paris, and in coming together in the radiance of universal benevolence, they were bestowing on the world a new sun and source of light.[4] As Tocqueville wrote, "No one doubted that the fate of mankind was involved in what was about to be done."[5] This feeling found echoes abroad: "It seems to me," wrote Fichte in 1793, "that the French Revolution affects the whole human race."[6]

The solar myth of the Revolution is one of those collective imaginings that are widespread just because they are so general and vague. Perhaps, in 1789, it owed much of its intensity to the fact that it enabled people, in the heat of their temporary rapture, to overlook the concrete problems involved in organizing society. It existed at a level of consciousness at which fact is interpreted at the same time as a new reality is brought into being. It was at once an imaginative reading of a moment in history and a creative act that helped to change the course of events. I am convinced that in this mythical image we touch upon a central and seminal fact which enables us to deal in parallel with a number of ideas and events and works of art whose kinship is made evident by the metaphorical factor they have in common. The simple image of the triumph of light, and of a source and origin, is a key image.[7]

Let us try to define more clearly the nature of the myth and its effects. While it is true that the disintegration of the Ancien Régime was reflected in the passion to end everything which drew such emblematic figures as Don Juan and Valmont toward self-destruction, we should not forget a converse and complementary passion—the passion for beginning, or beginning again. In some people both passions may have existed, either together or one after the other; or they may have lent to the same penchant for violent action both its destructive and its creative aspects, in a contradiction more apparent than real. Indeed, all the evidence suggests that the same energy, the same radicalism, could be put to the service of both death and resurrection. Anything that is irrevocably wiped out leaves the way open for a beginning. Anything that begins gloriously rests upon a previous void and a past over and done with. Joseph de Maistre, an enemy of the Revolution, wrote: "If Providence rubs out, it is probable that it may write." Fichte, a supporter of the Revolution, expressed the interdependence between darkness and light by giving a 1793 political pamphlet, which hailed the advent of the new age, the dateline "Heliopolis, in the last year of darkness."[8] The deeper the night, the brighter will be Helios' rising.

12)   Louis Léopold Boilly (1761–1845). *The Triumph of Marat.*
(Lille, Musée des Beaux-Arts. Photo Giraudon)

Of course we must avoid confusion and distinguish between, on the one hand, the irresistible tendency of aristocratic libertines who sought their own annihilation in pleasure and dissipation and, on the other, the popular violence that attacked a strictly external enemy. In these cases, destructive energy is exercised in diametrically opposite directions. At first sight there seems to be nothing in common between the mortal fascination that drew the rake and the characters of Sade and the fury of the mobs who, driven by fear and want, destroyed the symbols of feudalism. But when we look closer we see a correspondence and complementarity amounting to an inversion and a transmutation. The life of a rake is made up of a discontinuous series of dazzling moments separated by dark intervals: It is finally swallowed up in death. The revolutionary consciousness, on the other hand, likes to begin with a swift and decisive act of destruction which it hopes will give rise to a continuous emission of light. The signs are reversed. Wealth, which the libertine needs to sustain his pleasures, is in correlation to the poverty of the people. The dark power of want, famine, and destitution is the shadow cast by the exclusive delights of the privileged. Because he is a prey to the dark drive of want, a poor man paradoxically identifies the brilliant life of the aristocrat with the blackness of a storm cloud. Whence a strange convergence: The man of pleasure rushing to his doom collides with a famished people hurling itself on the hated citadels. At the meeting point of these two forces beats the black heart of the Revolution and there ferments its fertile chaos (fig. 13). Here is the symbolic home of regicide; the bright star of the new age is only its replica in reverse.

13) JACQUES-LOUIS DAVID (1748–1825).
Marie Antoinette Being Led to Her Execution. 1793.
(Paris, Musée du Louvre. Photo Musées Nationaux)

After destruction, what emerges is empty space, a free horizon. The world of feudalism had sanctioned difference and had erected in human relations a whole system of compartments, grades, and distinctions that were symbols of qualitative difference and signs of the protection once afforded by the sovereign to his vassal. The protection had gone, but inequality of condition still existed, with all that it entailed of insult and humiliation for the inferior classes. So unjustified separations survived, absurd prohibitions, and barriers that merely excluded most people from the full enjoyment of the "natural" rights inherent in human life. This space, bristling with futile obstacles many of which were already falling into ruin, was just waiting to be cleared, to be made homogeneous and "isotropic" like the space of the new celestial mechanics, open in all directions to the universal force of gravity.[9] One result of revolutionary violence was this vast opening up of space, the creation of this unified field in which enlightenment and law could spread out in all directions.

When he charged the three orders to present their credentials and pursue their deliberations separately, Louis XVI was faithfully interpreting the spirit of feudalism, the aim of which was to divide society into unalterably distinct sections. But the Third Estate immediately saw itself as the expression of the whole nation. It offered admission to members of the nobility and clergy who wanted to join the Commons. It declared itself a National Assembly and concentrated its whole attention on drawing up, on the American model, a declaration affecting the entire human race. In all these actions the Third Estate was following the ideal of a homogeneous whole. Its task was to arrive at a comprehensive definition of one law for all men and of equality for all men before the law.

The same consideration explains the anticlericalism of the Revolution. It was directed not so much against the religious idea as such as against the church as a temporal power whose wealth and privileges made it an inadequate mediator between man and God. Secularization and expropriation were generally aimed not at abolishing religious feeling but rather at restoring to the relations between man and God the same immediacy as the political revolution aimed at establishing between all people. Tocqueville saw that this was a rediscovery of the spirit of religious universalism, but with the object now of applying its consequences on earth:

> The French Revolution, in relation to this world, operated in exactly the same way as religious revolutions operate in relation to the other. It looked at the citizen in abstract terms, independent of different societies, just as religions look at man in general independent of country and date. It sought not only the special right of the citizen of France but the political rights and duties of men in general.
>
> It was by thus going back always to what was least particular, what was so to speak most *natural* as regards society and government, that the Revolution made itself understandable to all and imitable in a hundred places at once.[10]

PRINCIPLES

AND

WILL

T HE FIRST act of freedom clears the way and opens up a limitless field of possibility. But no one can remain forever on this momentary crest, when darkness rolls away and the light of the future presents all faces because it as yet has none. The new space has to be filled, the god who will be at its center has to be named, the power that is to rule it has to be recognized or created. The fact of having darkly overthrown the reign of darkness determines only a possibility of beginning and not the nature of what is going to begin. All that emerges at first is the fact that the field is open to universal principles. For a principle is the word of beginning, the founding utterance that tries to contain and fix in itself beginning's bright authority. The nothing in which debauchery ends must give birth to resolute virtue.

The entire age set itself to going back to and clearly formulating principles. The language of principles had been established long before 1789, and with the approach of the meeting of the States General theoretical writings proliferated, each more dogmatic than the last. "*Tutti soloneggianno i Parigini*" ("All the Parisians are playing Solon") jested Alfieri in a letter to André Chénier on April 29, 1789. When the ship of traditional monarchy foundered, anyone who could hold a pen set up as a lawmaker. The white light of the first moments of the Revolution was perhaps only the eddying of all the colors in the spectrum of principles, whirling round in the space won at last by freedom. It has often been pointed out that while some of the Revolution's aims were inspired by England or America or what people imagined to be the early institutions of the French monarchy, most of them were built up in the abstract, on the basis of a tabula rasa that authorized the reconstruction of everything on the first legitimate foundations of social existence. Were these various ideas, all magnanimous, all quite plausible on the level of theory, doomed to be nothing more than an unverifiable reflection of their authors' own private convictions? By what magic was thought going to become something more than this intangible discourse, this fine and limpid chain of argument exposed to the infinite possibility of contradiction? In fact, for principles to assert themselves, spread, and leave a trace in the world, thought had to enter into an alliance with an effective agent, an additional force. In other words, instead of speculative reason staying isolated in the order of ideas, it needed to be reinforced by an intense and passionate energy: Its very expansion depended on it. Here the lesson taught by Rousseau was to become a determining factor and meet with an enthusiastic welcome.[1] Rousseau's work, though based on solitude, demonstrated with a remarkably widespread and penetrating influence a fertile alliance between the power of thought and the warm impulse of passion. Let me remind readers of the fascination exercised by that accusing eloquence in which thought and feeling vie with each other: Doctrine takes on the urgency of an appeal, while passion looms larger and clearer in a wide-ranging rational discourse. Rousseau aims at destroying all authority imposed from without. He urges his readers to obey an authority which is not that of speculative reason but that of practical reason in its collective aspect, that is, the general will. He follows the same method in expounding his religion and morality, where everything is based on the evidence of inner feeling, a faculty which precedes reason but which even the strictest reason cannot deny. When the boldest deputies of the Third Estate adopted the language of Rousseau they ceased to be thinkers trying to demonstrate the idea of a pact of association: Under the pressure of circumstance and by a sort of *petitio principii*, or begging of the question, they ascribed absolute and undeniable antecedence to the collective ego of the nation. Their presence in Versailles, their claims, their constitutional systems were already both expressions and acts of popular sovereignty. It was a matter no longer of debating its intellectual validity but of putting it into practice. They were moved and activated by it; they were its agents and tools. The decrees they passed no longer sought to prove the theoretical truth of the general will: They were willed by it; it was already sovereign, and irrefutably at work in them. Here we see the full significance of Mirabeau's reply to the marquis de Dreux-Brézé—it matters little whether the story is true or apocryphal: "Tell those who sent you we are here by the *will* of the people, and that we shall not leave our places except by the force of the bayonet."[2]

What Mirabeau said and did on this occasion was not didactic in tone or performed with speculative calm. Principles and will were mingled and made indistinguishable. Mirabeau's own will claimed to be identical with the national will. And memorable events took place at the point where this will-cum-principle confronted the ill-will, the individual will, which tried to resist it and which, by instructing the States to "deliberate in separate orders," ignored the universality of the general will.

And thus it was that principles entered into the reality of history. The discourse of reason, swept along by the passion of the will, sought an entry into the world, a vessel to receive it. The great moments of the Revolution are episodes in this incarnation: From this point on we see the discourse of reason only as it is alloyed with the tension of the wills of men of action and with the incidental resistance of the preexisting world. Admittedly, it was a reason that was buried and more or less diverted from its aim, but it was also materiality raised to the power of a symbol.

Up to the death of Robespierre the Revolution unfolded in a symbolic language out of which its legend was made, in which modern exact inquiry tries to discover the play of the "real" forces involved. Crowd reactions, festivities, and emblems are the elements that go to make up this symbolic discourse, which taken as a whole both conceals and reveals a decisive step in history. They are elements that form part of reality.

To express the matter in a rather bold generalization, this symbolic history may be interpreted in terms of the glory and tribulation of light. Will and revolutionary principles tended to spread everywhere and to assemble people in a common space, one and indivisible, in which reigned openheartedness and civic fervor. It probably received its fullest expression in the great ceremonial of the Feast of the Federation on July 14, 1790. But when reason descends into reality it descends into opaqueness.

The Revolution owed its success, its rhythm, its catastrophic acceleration, to an unforeseen coalition between light, or enlightened reformism, on the one hand, and, on the other, the dim impetus of the angry mobs. It is the history of a way of thinking which, as it passed into action, was taken over, boosted, and overtaken by a violence it had not anticipated; it tried to decipher the meaning of this violence and to control the reactions it provoked in the authoritarian language of proclamations and decrees. This produced the complex confrontation that constitutes the inner law of the Revolution. The geometrical blueprints and the principles worked out by speculative reason did not have a clear field; the violence that arose out of dark destitution and ancient anger could express itself only in the primitive form of destruction. The revolutionary act is a synthesis of these two opposite terms: In it, principles enter into facts as part of the same movement as that which hoists hitherto dumb violence to the level of language. The language of theory and principle had to enter into an alliance and a compromise with an element of darkness and passion, of fear and fury; with the violence of the basic misery and want that drove the raging mobs. No matter how lucidly legitimate order was demonstrated in theory, it remained powerless until it took on the force of law and won recognition and acceptance as a viable institution. It has to impose its own necessity as against the opposing necessity of poverty and violence. In order to interpret, dominate, direct, and contain those dark forces, language would try to attain its maximum efficiency, its utmost energy. It would become oracular, sententious, prophetic. The laconic, paroxysmal eloquence seems like an attempt to win people's minds by a sort of magic: Its aim is not so much to explain events as to create them through a demiurgic act. In its attempt to lend principles the force that makes them effective, language let itself be annexed by the violence it sought to tame. Without losing any of its brilliance, the limpid speech of principle became the trenchant words of action. It was no longer to be compared with the innocent transparency of crystal but with the cutting edge of steel. To expound the source of the law was no longer enough; now those who opposed it had also to be punished. Obviously, there was a risk that this sort of language would wear itself out in an ever-mounting tide of austere vehemence, anathema, and unrelenting abstraction.

The same will that determined the progress of the Revolution, as soon as it could no longer be regarded with certainty as an emanation of the general will (and there was no absolute proof to support such certainty), became increasingly threatened by an invading darkness: Would it let itself be overwhelmed by the confused exaltation of dissidence and its claims and of personal greed? Before long it had become a dark and "factious" will, which instead of working for unity was splintering and fomenting division. The light of the Revolution that had been born of the rolling back of darkness now had to confront the return of darkness, which threatened its inmost being. In attempting to enter into the world, it had encountered a resistance made up of the inertia of things and of the opposing will of those who refused to accept the new truth. Theoretical reason and the enthusiasm that dissemi-

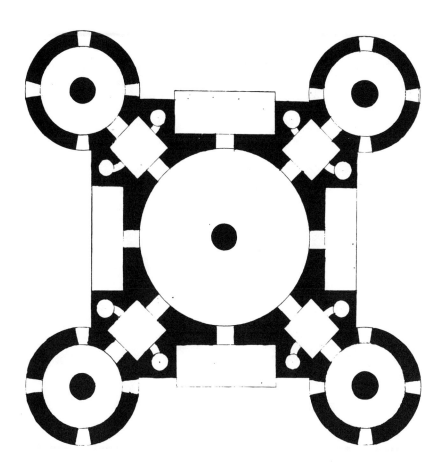

14) Louis-Jean Desprez (1743–1804). State Prison.
    (Stockholm, Kungliga Biblioteket)

nated it had to face the play of "real forces." Thus they
would witness the rebirth of the dark enemy whom
they would have liked to be rid of once and for all. Any
delay in the march toward enlightenment, any holdup
in the practical organization of the revolutionary State,

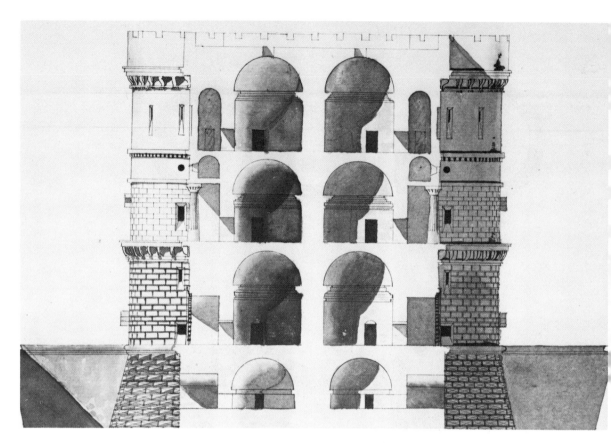

15) LOUIS-JEAN DESPREZ (1743–1804). State Prison.
(Stockholm, Kungliga Biblioteket)

was attributed (often with good reason) to counter-revolutionaries, conspirators, or agents of the enemy coalition. By trying to establish the reign of virtue, revolutionary reason made the reign of suspicion inevitable, and, soon after, the reign of terror. It had to keep on repeating the act of violence, the inaugural act by which light triumphed over darkness. The capture of the Bastille had not been a sufficient dawn. Darkness and sin still had to be punished in the person of the king himself. Lebrun celebrated the execution of Louis

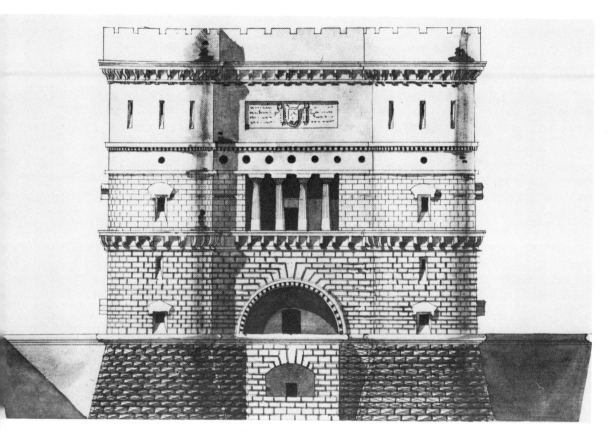

16) LOUIS-JEAN DESPREZ (1743–1804). State Prison.
(Stockholm, Kungliga Biblioteket)

Capet with the lines

> Centuries of servitude, one day breaks your fetters!
> The usurping scepter is succeeded by a just empire.
> Republic, you are born to avenge the whole uni-
> verse.[3]

The act of regicide should have been the highest
point and absolute symbol of this repeated negation
and avenging awakening: It was not, because resistance to the revolutionary ideal found a providential

LA LIBERTÉ

17 PIERRE-PAUL PRUD'HON (1758–1823). *Liberty*,
engraved by Copia.
(Phot. Bibl. nat. Paris)

support in the very bloodshed that was supposed to
signify the advent of a new age. The Terror shows the
revolutionary will at grips with a counterwill—one

both real and imaginary, projected and introjected. It had been a mistake to think that the light of the Revolution could impose itself on the world at a single blow and with just one irruption: When France was in danger, and under the Committee of Public Safety, the struggle emerged as a permanent one, with victory forever postponed. The Terror was a long celebration of sacrifice and new birth, but in it freedom, caught up in the fascination of anarchy, was unable to take on the fixed form that had been hoped for. It would be going too far to say that Thermidor and the death of Robespierre marked the failure of the revolutionary will. But thereafter will and principle were no longer in such close alliance, and sometimes even broke with one another. When it encountered obstacles the language of principles became eroded and distorted, and the meaning of words was impoverished or obscured. There are many witnesses to the fact that after 1794 language was jaded. Allegories lost their power, and people soon began to object to mystification. Quite apart from the cause it helped to defend, the following passage, written by Benjamin Constant in 1814, may serve as a general diagnosis of people's state of mind under the Directory:

> In all violent struggles, interests follow in the path of high-flown ideas just as birds of prey flock after armies about to do battle. Hatred, revenge, greed, and ingratitude shamelessly parodied the noblest examples because they had been crudely exhorted to imitate them. Treacherous friends, dishonest debtors, secret informers, and venal judges all found their justification written in advance in conventional language. Patriotism became the readymade excuse for every crime. Great sacri-

fices, acts of devotion, victories won by the stern republican-
ism of Antiquity over natural inclination—these merely
served as a pretext for the reckless unleashing of selfish passions.

[*De l'esprit de conquête et de l'usurpation, VIII*]

Behind the facade of principle lay appetite and self-
interest: It was becoming an age of "pragmatism."
Naked will still remained, but it was will without principle or based on principles suited to the occasion. Out
of all the principles worked out in the abstract by the
theorists of 1789, those that survived were such as
were convenient to the new ruling class. The play over,
masks and togas were thrown aside.[4] The mythology
of light and virtue was out of date: The country had to
be governed, even though by a Corsican general. Both
in France and elsewhere some of those who had hailed
the Revolution as a burst of light saw Bonaparte as a
prince of darkness. The reason of the Revolution would
belatedly produce a civil code and a completely central-
ized administration. But the effect of the revolutionary
will would only turn France into a short-lived empire,
arousing against her the rival wills of the other nations
of Europe, awakened in their turn to "patriotic" awareness. It is probable that the Napoleonic will was a *will
to law* because of its revolutionary antecedents. But
what it was remembered for was not so much law as
the exaggerated affirmation of will itself. What was to
emerge in nineteenth-century Europe as the ultimate
consequence and final betrayal of revolutionary thought
was the *will to will*, the will to power, the dark will that
refused to make common cause with the light of reason,
which it regarded, superficially, as "superficial."

THE

GEOMETRICAL

CITY

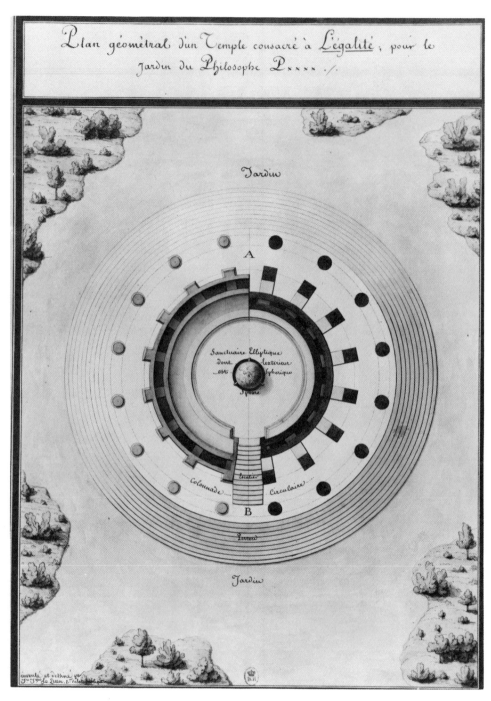

Plan géométral d'un Temple consacré à L'égalité, pour le Jardin du Philosophe P××××.

Jardin

A

Sanctuaire Elliptique dont l'extérieur est Sphérique

Sphère

Colonnade Circulaire

escalier

B

Perron

Jardin

inventé et dessiné par Jn Jqes Le Queu

18) JEAN-JACQUES LEQUEU (1757?–1825).
Ground plan of a temple consecrated to Equality.
(Phot. Bibl. nat. Paris)

W E HAVE already drawn a diagram of the fate of the Revolution in terms of the symbols used by the revolutionary age itself, and largely in relation to its art. But we should beware of seeking facile parallels between the history of the revolutionary endeavor and the development of art.[1] The main thing is to retain as guides and indicators such key ideas as that of light confronting darkness, the passion for beginning, and the union of principle and will.

Some of the pre-1789 writers who drew up principles for a perfect society complemented political doctrine with novels about government. They felt a need to add images to ideals, to plan an ideal city. Like all Utopian cities, theirs was based on the laws of a simple and rigid geometry. Its regular quandrangular or circular form made it divisible into either strictly equal juxtaposed parts or similarly symmetrical rings arranged round an omnipotent center: Equality in independence alternated with equality in dependence. It was as if the great ideas of equality by nature and equality before the law could be given immediate spatial expression by means of rule and compass. In a universe of signs, geometry was the language of reason.[2] It made use of forms of every kind in their beginning, their principle, and applied them in a system of points, lines, and constant proportions. Any excess or irregularity appeared as an intrusion of evil: Advocates of Utopia avoid superfluity. The principle of utility was concerned only with the fundamental needs imposed

[69]

by nature, not with those arising out of a corrupt civilization. And so there was no decoration, no luxury, no extravagant ornament. And so also Fichte used the image of the regular building at the same time as that of the victory of light: "The old robber châteaus are tumbling down on all sides. If we are left alone, they will become more and more deserted and abandoned to the birds that are the enemies of light, and to the bats and the owls. New buildings, on the other hand, will gradually spread until in the end they form a regular whole."[3]

Such were the somewhat sketchy architecture and town planning that pleased Utopian authors and armchair reformers. But what about the real architects and the professionals? There were some who went along with the amateurs and also returned to geometry in their plans and even in their actual constructions. Though they seem to us to have been inspired by dreams, they refused to dream lightly. Their imagination rejected the frivolities that had delighted previous generations; what they aspired to was simplicity, grandeur, and purity of taste. Dream and imagination tended to remove and tone down rather than multiply invented detail. After the decorative climax of rococo, it was frugality, hard-won, that produced a thrill. There was one contemporary of this striving for simplification, Joubert, who wrote: "Lines. Beautiful lines. Lines, the foundation of all beauty; architecture, for example; architecture is content to decorate them."[4] Even this decoration disappeared in the major projects of Boullée, Ledoux, and Poyet, which display pure forms—cubes, cylinders, spheres, cones, and pyra-

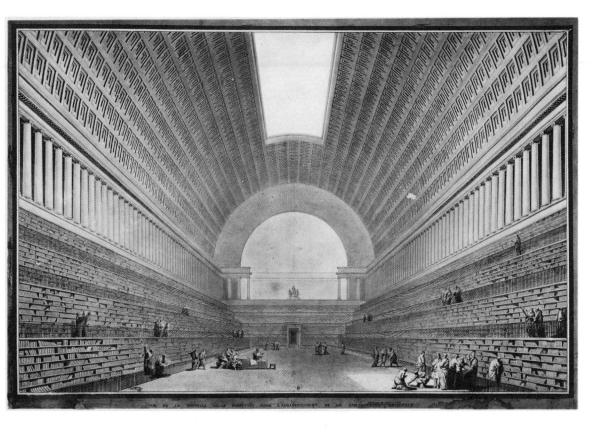

19) ETIENNE-LOUIS BOULLÉE (1728–1799).
Project for a national library. 1788.
(Phot. Bibl. nat. Paris)

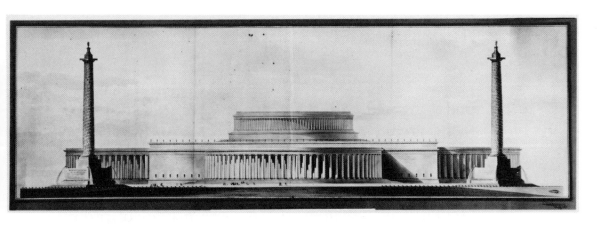

20) ETIENNE-LOUIS BOULLÉE (1728–1799).
Project for a museum.
(Phot. Bibl. nat. Paris)

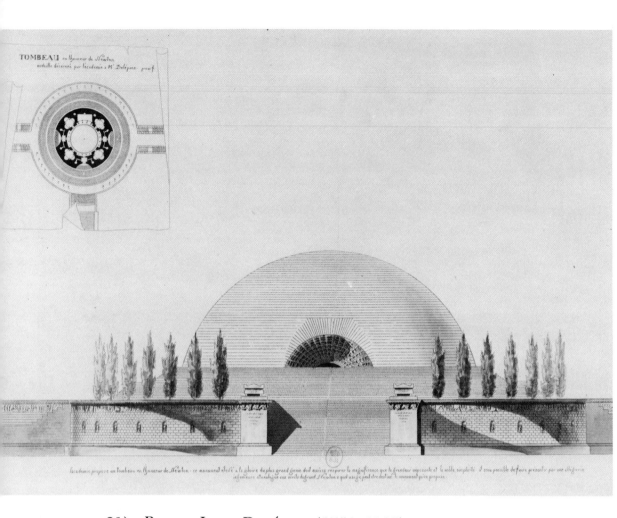

21) PIERRE-JULES DELÉPINE (1756–1835).
Tomb in honor of Newton. 1780?–1785.
(Phot. Bibl. nat. Paris)

mids—treated with both economy and elegance. With
them, architecture tried to go back to its basic functional truths and constituent elements. "The circle and
the square," wrote Ledoux, "are the alphabet authors
use in the texture of the best works."[5] Reaction against
buildings of the previous age was a kind of protest

[72]

against masks and untruth: Ornament had too long hidden essential structure, which was made beautiful by simple necessity. Stone, the raw material of architecture, had been treated as something alien, to be fretted and hollowed out like wood. This complaint had been voiced by certain theorists several decades earlier: It had been one of Lodoli's main themes. And Ledoux wrote: "We should mistrust those flaccidly produced lines, those forms broken up from the outset which are crushed beneath the weight of false taste, those cornices writhing like reptiles in the desert." Instead, stone, restored to its own truth "at the touch of art, will arouse a new feeling and develop its own qualities."[6] In this conversion, restoring architecture to its basic figures, and raw materials to their true nature, may be seen a choice that is moral as well as aesthetic. Just as stone was to become stone again, and a wall was to be once more a flat and almost naked surface, so man was to regain the fullness and simplicity of his own nature. The ideal of restored truth applied jointly to the human heart and to the buildings conceived of by the mind of the architect.[7] The moralizing appeal in the theoretical writings of Boullée and Ledoux was not an accidental adjunct, due to the contamination of contemporary "sensibility"; it was the actual purpose of what they were doing, shown by the way they made architecture into an eloquent pedagogy designed to save man from degradation. It was more than a pedagogy—it was a "demiurgy."[8] In an age when the divinity was thought of as a great architect, the human architect saw himself as a god and universal legislator. He arrogated to himself the power of rationally organizing material space and soon added to that power its full moral potential, making it in fact the power of transforming the whole world of man. The genius of the architect knew no bounds. "In his extensive view," wrote Ledoux, "everything comes within his sphere—politics, morals, law, religion, and government."[9] Quatremère de Quincy, who was far from completely sharing the audacious views of the "revolutionary" architects, used ethical terminology, in 1798, to criticize the faults of *bizarrerie*, by which he meant architectural whimsicality and extravagance:

> *Bizarrerie* implies an incurably immoral use of form. . . .[It] gives rise to a system destructive of order and of the forms prescribed by nature; [it] attacks the forms that go to make up art. . . . Experience has shown that this taste usually arises out of weariness of what is best; it has shown that, with nations as with individuals, it often comes from the satiety produced by abundance itself; and that it is in the midst of wealth and enjoyment of all kinds that there grows up this deadly aversion which poisons pleasure, makes the simple beauties of nature seem insipid, and requires the disguise of that perfidious art which aims not so much at satisfying as at stimulating or cheating desire. . . . Introduced into architecture, *bizarrerie* was able to exercise its power on a large scale. . . . straight lines were replaced by convolutions; severe outlines by undulations; regular plans by overelaborate, mixtilinear designs; the symmetrical by the picturesque; and order by the confusion of chaos.[10]

Borromini and his followers were held mainly responsible for these malpractices.

Quatremère de Quincy himself puts forward harmonious relationships "of the whole to the parts and of each part to the whole" as the condition of a grandeur which he qualifies sometimes as "proportional" and sometimes as "moral." True, he is not an out-and-out advocate of "mathematical simplicity," but he cannot help somehow connecting the idea of virtuous effort with that of harmonious relationship between the parts. "To produce an effect of grandeur, the object in which it is to inhere must be simple enough to strike us at a glance, that is to say in its entirety, and at the same time to strike us by the relations between its parts. Too frequent a repetition of small impressions would never produce the idea of grandeur. Our minds must be brought to make an effort to encompass the idea of dimension, and too many divisions diminish instead of increasing that power in us."[11]

The same author also refers to moral grandeur as ideal grandeur. It can be found in a small building if that building's proportions are perfect. It is so closely linked to perfection of relationship that dimension ("linear or dimensional grandeur") is unnecessary. But there is nothing to prevent dimensional and moral grandeur from existing together, and when they do a feeling of exaltation is offered to human awareness. When principles—that is, the harmony of elementary forms—are united with material grandeur, we reach the apogee which in the Revolution itself appeared as the wished-for fusion between the principles of universal law and the power of effective will. "In the works of nature the grandeur of mass pleases us because it makes us humble, and because the sense of our own littleness enlarges the soul by directing it toward the principle of all greatness. In the works of architecture the grandeur of mass pleases us because it makes us proud; man is proud to feel small beside the work of his own hands. He rejoices in the idea of his strength and power."[12] This was a different enjoyment from that pursued by the "*libertins*" of the Ancien Régime—the brief novelty of sensation which is soon exhausted and which *bizarrerie* strove to reawaken. Instead, this was a reflexive grasping of a power which shines out in splendor when man shows that he can harmonize number, primitive forms, moral virtue, and matter at once dominated and respected in its physical truth. A "nouveau régime" of sensibility was beginning, which set aside multiplicity of sensation in favor of the unity of one great spiritual intuition. This would only have been a revival of the more or less Platonic theory of the sixteenth and seventeenth centuries, except that now the notions of force and energy inclined idealism toward a determinedly modern voluntarism. The new doctrine disapproved of baroque and rococo as the art of the ephemeral, stimulating fleeting impressions according to the inconstant whim of fashion. The new view wanted architecture to become an art of permanence once more and wanted man to recognize in that permanence not only the authority of simple and eternal geometrical forms but also the edict of a mind that had left its own massive mark upon things and their duration in time.

But we should avoid giving an oversimplified picture of this simplicity-loving architecture. According to the approach one adopts, one can find in the work of someone like Ledoux now an inclination to individualize masses (which may be seen as a feature of modern individualism), now a desire to promote community

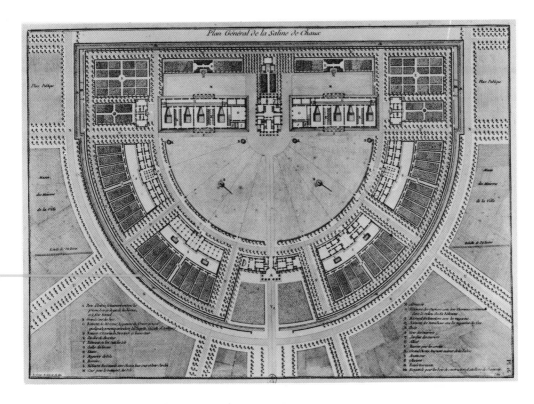

22) CLAUDE-NICOLAS LEDOUX (1736–1806).
General plan of the saltworks at Chaux.
(Phot. Bibl. nat. Paris)

life and centralized administration (this especially in the radial plan for the town of Chaux). In his plan for the Newton cenotaph, Boullée puts a representation of the sun in the middle of the sphere, with the idea of subordinating the whole edifice to the centrality of the principle of light and to the irresistible diffusion of its rays. But it was also Boullée who, wishing to express "immutability," dreamed of rivaling the pyramids and hypogea of the Egyptians: His plans set out the conditions necessary for a "buried architecture" and for an "architecture for the shades." In order to conjure up the fascinating melancholy beloved of his contemporaries,

[77]

23) ETIENNE-LOUIS BOULLÉE (1728–1799). Newton's cenotaph.
(Phot. Bibl. nat. Paris)

he intended to imitate "all that is gloomiest in nature."[13] It was as if the straight edges of large buildings, strictly dividing the lighted face from the dark one, made Boullée pay almost equal attention to the achievements of light and the resources of shade. So we are not surprised to find Boullée, driven by a lyricism that was more pictorial than architectural, producing, in his studies for the solar temple that was to be the Newton cenotaph, external views as seen both by day and by night. Baroque and rococo architecture, with its undulations and other "affected" or "mannered" forms, had provided transitions, gradations, and interactions between light and shadows. Baroque architects, often rivaling painters, adopted a scenographic approach to even their most durable constructions, inventing or organizing a complex organism in which contraries were married with each other rather than contrasted. But in the new spirit of geometrical architecture, opposition prevailed: The absolute rigor of forms set down by reason generates masses of homogeneous shadows, volumes in which night is held captive, dominated by the mastery and sharp determination of line. But one has the feeling that shade, thus liberated, purified and concentrated, might secede and create its own separate kingdom. In the "sepulchral" style we recognize a legacy from the "funeral" mode indulged in by baroque; but now the darkness is more oppressive and menacing: The tombs of Desprez, like the underground vaults of the Gothic novel (*roman noir*) and the châteaus of Sade's imagination, speak of a blackness that takes on a new meaning through its contrast with the white light of the law of day.

VUE INTÉRIEURE DU CÉNOTAPHE DE NEWTON

24) Etienne-Louis Boullée (1728–1799).
Newton's cenotaph, interior view, by night.
(Phot. Bibl. nat. Paris)

What was to be the function of the center in the regular geometry of circle and sphere? We might expect it to constitute a beneficent principle reigning supreme over the whole, as in the luminous globe of the Newton cenotaph, the chapel in Poyet's circular hos-

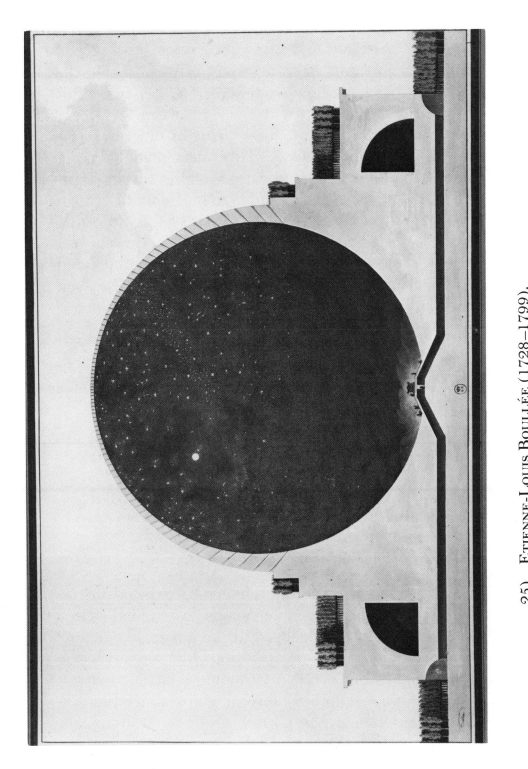

25) ETIENNE-LOUIS BOULLÉE (1728–1799).
Newton's cenotaph, section.
(Phot. Bibl. nat. Paris)

pital with corridors like the spokes of a wheel, and the director's house in the town designed by Ledoux.[14] But by a reversal consistent with the logic of the Terror, the center may be consecrated by virtue of suffering: The scaffold on which Louis XVI was decapitated was set up in the middle of the place des Victoires, the ambiguous point where the new light of the Republic was to be born out of the symbolic murder of the old order. The idea of a "dark center" was much in evidence in certain projects inspired by the Terror; these included a crematorium where a central flame could be seen burning like a power of destruction. Michelet wrote:

> One architect . . . invented a building for burning the dead which would have simplified everything. His plan was really striking. Imagine a vast, open, circular portico with pilasters forming arcades, under each of which was an urn containing ashes. In the middle was a tall pyramid emitting smoke from the top in all directions. It was an immense chemical apparatus which, without disgust and without horror, shortening the process of nature, would have taken a whole nation if necessary, and from the unquiet, unhealthy, polluted state called life would have conveyed them through pure flame to the peaceful state of final repose.

> [*La Revolution*, Book 21, chapter 1]

All this great style of architecture reduced to the simple principles of geometry was expounded like a plan but remained unrealized. Its language, like that of principles and social regeneration, had already been formulated before 1789. A harmonious city, a town for the beginning of an age, auroral, colossal, irrefutable, was to be found in the portfolios of several architects long before the taking of the Bastille. The Revolution

26) Louis-Jean Desprez (1743–1804). Imaginary sepulchre.
(Phot. Bibl. nat. Paris)

would have neither the time nor the resources, nor
perhaps the temerity, to ask them to put their great
civic projects into practice. On the contrary, it remembered and reproached them for the expensive works
they had carried out for the authorities and the privileged of the Ancien Régime. Ledoux had lent his talent
to the building of the Paris tollgates, which attracted
the wrath of the people in 1789; their creator spent
some time in prison. The Revolution itself built little.

27) FRANÇOIS BARBIER (1768–1826).
Column house at Le Désert de Retz.
(Phot. Bibl. nat. Paris)

It set up the hemicycles for parliamentary debate, in which, by the geometrical virtue of the diameter, there was soon invented the classic distinction between "right" and "left." It converted to the service of a new religiosity some ecclesiastical edifices built at the end of the Ancien Régime: Soufflot's church of St. Geneviève became the Pantheon, with a pagan appearance that, like its new name, harked back to the monuments of Rome, rejecting the patronage of the French and Christian saint. But it lost its medieval and Parisian name only in order to "antiquate" more thoroughly the "great men" of France, to give a more heroic aura to those who were the nation's glory. To sober, simplify, and laicize the building, Quatremère de Quincy did away with the eastern towers.

Far from following the injunctions of Ledoux and Boullée, builders compromised, toning down their bolder measures with a decorative display borrowed from tradition. Emil Kaufmann, an expert in the problems of the period, sees this as a sign of retreat. "To appreciate this withdrawal in architecture," he writes, "all one has to do is compare the winners of the Grand Prix between 1779 and 1789 with those between 1791 and 1806. The earlier ones are full of life and revolutionary boldness; the later ones demonstrate the victory of feeble resurrectionism."[15] In architecture (and perhaps in other fields too), it was as if invention and innovation had been stronger in a context of imminence and hope; as if the revolutionary ideal was really to be sought before the actual Revolution and its consequences. That ideal was bound to become unclear in the very moment of its fulfillment: The necessity it

28) CLAUDE-NICOLAS LEDOUX (1736–1806).
Director's house, project for the city of Chaux.
(Phot. Bibl. nat. Paris)

29) CLAUDE-NICOLAS LEDOUX (1736–1806). Educational building.
(Phot. Bibl. nat. Paris)

claimed as its authority doomed it to be lost in the act of realization, betrayed and distorted not so much by its enemies as by those who tried to put it into practice. But it was a fruitful betrayal, the only way principles could be translated into facts, though one which forced the spirit of the Revolution to appear other in reality from what it had thought itself, and different from the aims which had originally inspired it. History is a battlefield where men struggle to make a new world corresponding to the stimulating images which moved them to change the old. When it abolished the feudal order, the Revolution set in motion a process that was to make equally obsolete the ideal figures and Utopian plans that had been brought into being, under the Ancien Régime, to oppose it. Such, Hegel would later tell us, is the irony of history.

SPEAKING

ARCHITECTURE,

WORDS MADE

ETERNAL

30)　Jean-Jacques Lequeu (1757–?1825).
Orthographic projection of the tomb of Lars Porsena,
king of Etruria. 1792.
(Phot. Bibl. nat. Paris)

I N THE new architecture, basic geometrical forms were adapted not only to the functional necessities of building but also to the conveying of meaning. As well as aiming at simplicity through a return to basic forms, the new architecture endeavored too to be "speaking," or eloquent, to organize these forms in such a way as to make their function externally evident. This ambition, seen first of all in the choice in favor of simplification and unadorned monumentality, went on to imprint every building with clues as to its practical purpose. Form served function, but function was in turn reflected in form, to make it manifest: To function itself was added a symbolism of function. In this way the will of the builder was revealed simultaneously as controlling power and finalizing energy. The grandeur of a building declared simultaneously its purpose and its significance. While interplay of form was subservient to utility, practical values too sought universal recognition through the medium of a decipherable language. In speaking architecture, utility was apparent to every eye, proclaiming itself of benefit to the common good. The aim of these architects, trying to make their works instantly legible, was to persuade the viewer that the particular utility of each building is part of the overall system of reciprocal services that goes to make up public utility (figs. 14, 31, 32). Neither the purpose of a building nor the commitment of its owner could be a private matter. They concerned everyone, and therefore had to be openly declared. But one has only to look at the works of Lequeu to see how easily speaking architecture could degenerate into garrulousness. Here discourse degenerates into dogma and fantasy: Symbol stiffens into allegory, emblems come oddly to life in a motley world that is sometimes poetic but often wildly so (figs. 30, 33). Once again geometry was overgrown.

But it was not enough merely to proclaim the supremacy of eternal principles—of Liberty, Equality, Justice, and Patriotism—and make them visible in stone and the massive majesty of monuments. These were but the material marks of a metaphysical permanence, the outward signs of a truth at last revealed and made manifest. Their supremacy became complete only when men, the whole human race, turned toward principles in a surge of exaltation and gratitude. The great emblems were rallying points attracting all sensitive souls and men of goodwill: Significance resided not so much in a building itself as in popular "support" for it. In its extreme iconoclasm, the spirit of 1789 abolished or simplified decoration, giving preeminence to human events and the coming together of citizens seeing themselves as equals in the light of the rejoicings uniting them. In 1790, on the anniversary of July 14, the Feast of the Federation assembled representatives of the whole of France—or rather of its "active citizens"—around an altar to the *Patrie*, or homeland, specially erected in the Champ-de-Mars. Citizens of both sexes and of all classes had helped in the preparatory digging. Cellérier, one of the best contemporary architects, had built a triple triumphal arch. The Bastille had been an obscure prison overwhelmed by a furious attack. But in its commemoration the symbol was sub-

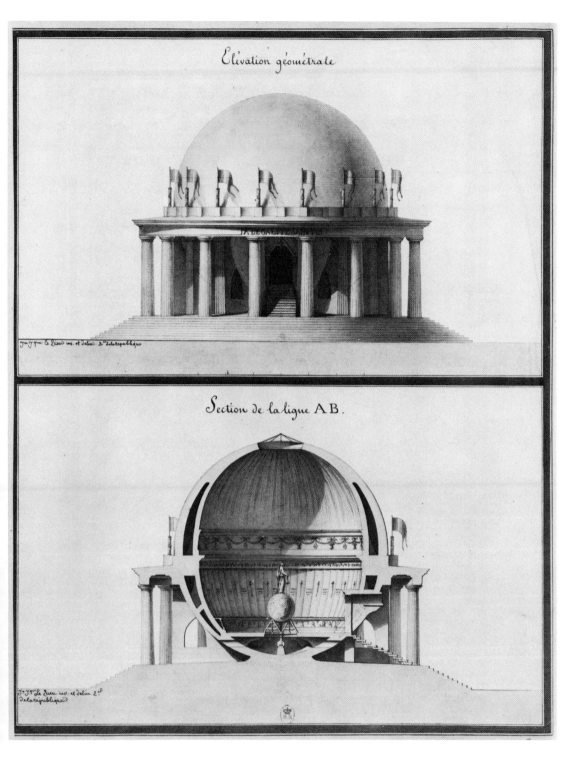

Élévation géométrale

Section de la ligne A.B.

31 + 32) JEAN-JACQUES LEQUEU (1757–?1825).
Temple consecrated to Equality.
(Phot. Bibl. nat. Paris)

33)　JEAN-JACQUES LEQUEU (1757–?1825).
Symbolic figure of a representative order,
Hall of State in a national palace. 1789.
(Phot. Bibl. nat. Paris)

limated, and the central altar to the *Patrie*, which com-
manded the rest, appealed to a contrasting emotion—
to fervor and enthusiasm. Once the sacred had exercised a negative fascination; now it was exhibited in its
positive aspect. Even more typical was the memorial
celebration on September 20, 1790, for those who had
died in Nancy. The architect, Ramée, erected a central
raised altar reached by a series of steps. Amid these
temporary arrangements, the flags, the bands, the
choirs, the cannon, and the processions formed a spectacle, a celebration that Michelet went so far as to relate
to a "new religion," in which the living proclaimed
their obedience to eternal principles. These were the
rites of a new subjection by which men, instead of
being bound by the whim of a single man, tyrant or
despot, were ruled over by the power of feeling and
reason which illuminated and supported the nature of
each individual and united him to other men. The vocabulary of the Revolution, like that of the philosophy
of the Enlightenment, showed considerable variations
on this point: Humanity, liberty, the homeland, the
Supreme Being were among the phrases used. But
whatever the terminology and however high the new
authority was placed, what was involved was always
a participatory subjection. Revolutionary celebrations
were solemn acts in which man paid homage to a divine
power that he had descried in himself. It was not a
religion dedicated to man but a lofty recognition of the
divine element present in every individual, the basis of
a communion in which rules were no longer imposed
from without but would be the result of a universal
spontaneity of conscience. Man honored a power that

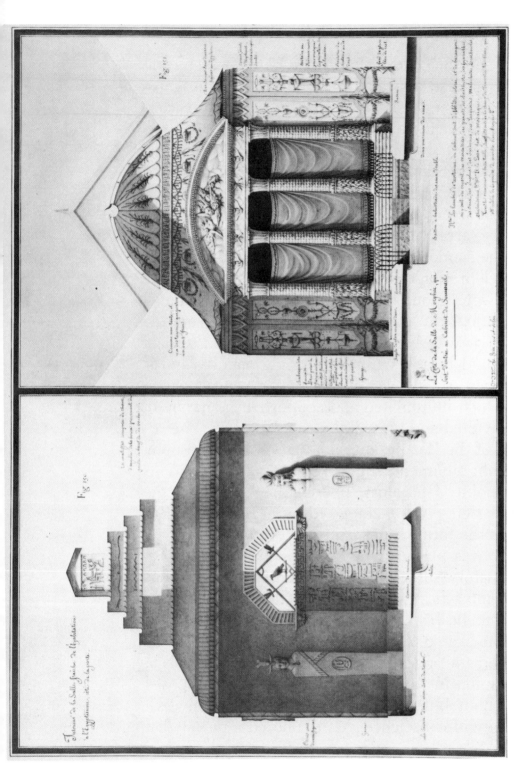

34) JEAN-JACQUES LEQUEU (1757–?1825).
Left, interior of the cool room of the Egyptian residence;
right, Morpheus room, which serves as an entrance hall to the sleep cabinet. (Phot. Bibl. nat. Paris)

35) JEAN-JACQUES LEQUEU (1757–?1825).
Top, the old castle by the sea; *bottom*, a wind pump.
(Phot. Bibl. nat. Paris)

surpassed but was not alien to him, a power from which he could not be divided, before which he need not humble himself, and whose service was no longer the privilege of a separate clergy. Each alike felt himself the repository of the new revelation, the agent of a new providence. The godhead inherent in each emerged more visibly when a crowd came together in single-mindedness. The supreme light, otherwise divided among individual minds, merged, by such concord, into a single radiance, thus re-creating the living image of the source of all things.

Because human life had a part in divinity, living men wanted to represent divinity in terms of life. The motionless images of ancient authority—statues of Christ, of the Virgin, of the saints, and of the kings of France—were knocked down or decapitated by revolutionary iconoclasm. They were no longer seen as containing something holy, and the stone itself was destroyed as an emblem of the old oppression, of a law dictated from above by impostors and tyrants. In their place, the revolutionary faith used as emblems living objects or people of flesh and blood: young trees, children placed on the altar, goddesses played by actresses. When Jacques-Louis David, exiled in Brussels under the Restoration, recalled the festivities he had designed, the images that came back to him were of youthful figures decked out in the noble finery of revived Antiquity: "Reason and Liberty enthroned in antique chariots, splendid women . . . the Greek line in all its purity, with beautiful girls in tunics, throwing flowers; and through it all the anthems of Lebrun, Méhul, and Rouget de Lisle."[1]

THE OATH:

DAVID

36) Jean Antoine Houdon (1741–1828).
George Washington. 1785.
(Paris, Musée du Louvre. Photo Musées Nationaux)

A REVOLUTIONARY celebration, organized in a special setting, was an event which though it lasted only one fleeting day aimed at marking an era. In this it differed from an aristocratic fete, an ephemeral brilliance that faded without leaving a trace. The revolutionary fete emerged as an act of foundation. It was an inaugurating communion; not a bright but evanescent foam on the waves of unstable time but a promise that the future would keep. The passage of time (soon marked by a calendar observing the requirements of reason and starting with the Year I of a new era) should produce a continuous line of loyalty. Some significant act was needed to mark the encounter between transient crowds and eternal principles, to seal the indissoluble bond which men contracted with one another and which they would make the starting point of a new alliance. An oath was such an act. It was a single act, a brief event, taking place in a fleeting moment; but it involved the future and united energies that would otherwise have been scattered. An aristocratic fete was lost in dizzy profusion, and the pleasure that lit it with a thousand separate lights burned for a moment only and then was swallowed up in darkness and oblivion. I see pleasure and oath as two moments governed by opposite signs. But the oath must be contrasted not only with pleasure but also with the traditional ceremony of the *sacre*, or anointing of the kings of France. Through an intervention from on high, in the name of a transcendent God, the coronation ceremony invested the monarch with the supernatural insignia of his power. The revolutionary oath created sovereignty, whereas the monarch received it from Heaven. The separate will of each individual became generalized as all pronounced the words of the oath: It was from the depths of every single life that the common utterance arose that would be the source of future law, at once impersonal and human.

The year 1789 saw the taking of many oaths. These included George Washington's oath of allegiance to the American Constitution on April 30; the Tennis Court Oath on June 20, when the deputies of the Third Estate declared themselves a National Assembly and swore not to separate until they had given France a constitution; and the oaths of the National Guards: "All national militia are to take the oath in the presence of their commanders . . . and all troops, that is to say officers of all ranks and soldiers alike, are to take an oath of loyalty to the Nation, and to the King, head of the Nation, with the highest solemnity." In the following year the civil constitution of the clergy required priests to swear loyalty to the Nation. After mass had been celebrated by Talleyrand, bishop of Autun, the Feast of the Federation on July 14, 1790, became one immense taking of the oath. Marriages were often celebrated before the altar to the *Patrie*, thus combining the loyalties of the spouse and of the citizen. And every flag, with its legend, "Liberty or Death," was a reminder of an oath.

The act of taking the oath, a physical moment of tension founding the future in the exaltation of a moment, was based on an antique model. At the same time as it inaugurated the future it also repeated a very

37) JOHANN HEINRICH FÜSSLI (1741–1825).
The Oath of the Three Swiss Guards. 1779–81.
(Kunsthaus Zürich)

ancient archetype for entering into a contract. The taking of the oath was a representation, a new actualization of this archetype, and the person taking the oath could not avoid seeing himself as an actor with a preexisting role, though that role now consisted in inventing a future. Moreover, since the values to which the oath pledged loyalty were supposed to be eternal, what was begun by the act of inauguration was really only a revival of a sovereignty that had been forgotten. In 1789 few people spoke of sweeping everything away in favor of what Barnave has called "total reconstruction": The words most frequently used were *regeneration* and *restoration*. People did not want to innovate; they wanted to go back to forgotten origins. (After the night of August 4, "the National Assembly solemnly proclaims King Louis XVI Restorer of the liberty of France.")

Between 1779 and 1781 J. H. Füssli (known in England as Fuseli) painted *The Oath of the Three Swiss Guards* (fig. 37). He brought the three figures together in a common gesture, with the three left arms held out horizontally and the joined hands forming the picture's central nexus. The men's raised right arms, and their eyes lifted heavenward, provided the vertical axes. The picture reflects Fuseli's admiration for Klopstock: The impulse of human solidarity is paralleled by an appeal to a protective transcendence, while the atmosphere is one of heroic elegance so strained it gives an impression of déjà vu. If the act of taking the oath was based on a previous model, so too the style of the painter echoed a previous art—the art of Michelangelo, Giulio Romano, and Marcantonio Raimondi.

In his *Oath of the Horatii* (1784–1785), Jacques-Louis David gave the subject its most powerful expression, and the one that best reveals the aesthetic climate of the time (fig. 38). The scene is Rome, in the early days of the Republic. The three Horatii swear, in the presence of their father, to defend the fatherland, the *Patrie*. This time the central point of the painting is the left hand of the old Horatio, lifting up the three swords that symbolically unite three wills. The father looks at the hilts of the swords, and it is toward the same point that the sons stretch out their arms; the eyes of the sons meet those of the father on the three separate yet united hilts, so that the focal point of the brothers' communion is the fasces, or sheaf, of death-dealing weapons sanctified by the paternal hand that proffers them. Here the vertical, which in Fuseli's picture is indicated by the upraised arms, is marked by the massive Doric columns in the background, and especially by the pike and the swords, together forming a pattern of opposing obliques. The sacred element resides in soldierly duty. (Not that David refused on principle to refer to a more distant transcendence, for he later organized the Feast of the Supreme Being, and in 1787 the protagonist in his *Death of Socrates* [fig. 39] is pointing toward Heaven.) So here, at the beginning of an age of conscription and national armies, we find the ancient legend of sacrifice for the fatherland being acted out in a symbolic setting. The father, looking not at his sons but at the arms he entrusts to them, holds victory dearer than the lives of his children. The sons, for their part, belong henceforward more to their oath than to themselves. The heroic impulse involves the leaving

38) JACQUES-LOUIS DAVID (1748–1825).
Oath of the Horatii. 1784–85.
(Paris, Musée du Louvre. Photo Musées Nationaux)

39) JACQUES-LOUIS DAVID (1748–1825).
The Death of Socrates. 1787.
(New York, The Metropolitan Museum of Art, Wolfe Fund, 1931)

behind of tangible attachments and natural bonds for the sake of an idea, an idea of which the father's hand is but a touching metaphor. But *The Oath of the Horatii* had to show the strength of immediate emotion, if only to indicate the distance set between it and themselves by the warriors vowed to death or victory. The group of women on the right expresses the helpless force of grief. This completes the dramatic demonstration in which firm masculinity, by which a man forgets himself in order to perform a mortal duty, is contrasted with sensitive femininity, which cannot face up to death and lets itself be overwhelmed by horror.

The same emotional contrast is not to be seen in David's great sketches for *The Tennis Court Oath* (fig. 40). Here the artist gives the Horatii's gesture to the assembled crowd of deputies, and this time the center of the composition is not a trio of swords but the written word—the proclamation being read aloud by Jean-Sylvain Bailly. The tension now is essentially more abstract, consisting in the relation between the individual image of each participant and the shifting unity of the whole. David *thinks* his picture, building it up out of great waves that are distributed harmonically; out of this mass of human beings he wants to make not a collective portrait but a set of individual ones. The only opponent to the proclamation—Martin Dauch, deputy for Castellane—is there in the picture, sitting with his arms folded on his chest (see the sketch in the museum at Versailles). The fact that David has given him this prominence—in order to expose him to disapproval—strengthens the allusion to individual conscience: The great collective impulse is in the first place the decision of each particular will. Another sketch for

The Tennis Court Oath presents the figures in the antique-style athletic nude, but gives their facial features a portraitlike accuracy. We are made to observe from life the problem of how to reconcile the ideal and the individual characteristic. In its clarity of drawing, its eloquent purity of pose, and in its "anatomical" beauty, the picture presents us with the ideal; but the faces, even if they reflect a noble transport rather than any other passion, present us with the characteristics of individual existence, the irregularities of a living Nature which loyalty to the art of imitation will not allow to be reduced to an "ideal" type. Compared with the problem David had to solve in the *Oath*, the composition of the *Coronation* of Napoleon seems very easy. In the sketches for the former, there is only one motionless figure—Dauch sitting unmoving on his chair. In the *Coronation*, the only movement is in the hands of Napoleon, raising the crown.

The great *Brutus* exhibited in the 1789 Salon reveals the other aspect of the oath and shows the extreme limit of patriotic devotion.[1] Its full title is *J. Brutus, first consul, returned home after having sentenced his two sons to death for joining the Tarquins and conspiring against Roman liberty. The lictors bring him their dead bodies for burial.* All this is necessary if the picture is to be fully understood. It represents the last moment of a tragedy, the moment when Alfieri brought down the curtain on his own *Bruto primo*, dedicated to George Washington in 1788.[2] In the play, while his colleagues and the people salute Brutus' "superhuman strength" and call him the "father" and "God" of Rome, Brutus describes himself as "the unhappiest man ever born."[3]

A collection of Alfieri's tragedies, in Italian, was

40) JACQUES-LOUIS DAVID (1748–1825).
The Tennis Court Oath. 1791.
(Musée de Versailles. Photo Musées Nationaux)

published in Paris in 1789, the year David completed his picture, and the artist was as much indebted to Alfieri as to Livy or Voltaire. And Chénier, another poet, was to write an ode on the Tennis Court Oath which refers to David's picture (literary painting indeed!) and speaks of

> The first consul, more citizen than father
> Returned home alone after passing sentence
> In homage to his beloved Rome
> And tasting the glorious pain that filled his heart.[4]

It is all over. The suffering yet inflexible father sits in the foreground, in the shadow, at the foot of a statue representing the deified homeland, *Dea Roma*. This emblem of the *Patrie*, backlighted, takes on the guise of a totem and stands between Brutus and the mutilated corpse which the lictors are bringing in in the background; a shaft of light falls on the body. The composition, in which everything is arranged according to the requirements of a discourse at once rational, allegorical, and emotive, shows that Brutus has put his country before the lives of his sons. The terrible higher life is concentrated in the statue of Rome, just glimpsed in the shadow: It is to her that the young men have been sacrificed, in a Roman, pagan version of the sacrifice of Abraham, a version in which no angel appeared to stay the father's hand. The oblique light that illuminates the corpse falls also on the group of women: The mother rises up in a great movement of desolation, while her two daughters cling to her, swooning. The picture contrasts masculine patriotism with feminine emotion, unmoving firmness and involuntary impulse,

and David distributed light and shade so as to bring
out the dramatic comparisons. He had freed himself of
the "flickering" lights that had tempted him when he
was still under the influence of the rococo masters; he
had renounced the masses of shadow that had temporarily attracted him in the Caravaggesques. Brutus, in
the half light, expresses the energy of considered determination, able to bear the consequences of his own
obedience to principle and so severe on disobedience as
to order the shedding of his own blood. It is himself,
his male posterity, that Brutus has sacrificed in having
his sons slain. In his hand he holds a scrap of parchment
that may or may not be the order of execution: In any
case, it is a page on which a sentence is written so that
it may endure. This mysterious text is the symbolic
counterpart of the workbasket on the table in the right-
hand part of the picture, which stands for a whole
world of patience and peace. The tragedy of history—
like the Revolution—has just invaded a human dwell-
ing, and the values and habits of private life have suddenly ceased to form a sheltered world apart. The
marvelous workbasket, with its innocent presence (forgotten by the actors in the tragedy and made evident
only to us, as witnesses), is a silent victim, a still life in
which the steel of the scissors symbolizes omnipresent
cruelty. It stands in the middle of the table, an article of
no importance, but pathetic in its very unimportance:
It is offered to our material perception as an image of
the "objective" universe from which the painter cannot
turn away. He contemplates the basket, and makes us
contemplate it, while his main aim is to make us see,
through tragic sublimity and Kantian dread, the moral

dimension in which a stricken man emerges as greater than his own destiny. The light, as well as awakening color, brings out aspects of the immediate: the corpse, in its immediacy as a body reduced to a thing; emotion, in the form of sudden start and helpless swoon. As Jean Leymarie has justly observed, "As in the *Horatii*, David concentrates his plastic energy on the manly Cornelian groups, and keeps his pictorial tenderness for the touching Racinian evocation of the women and children."[5] The power of drawing and line thus predominates in the depicting of the heroic character in whom feeling is subordinated to considered action. In the group of women, no less rigorously drawn and equally indebted to antique models, color is nevertheless given freer rein, so that pictorial values are linked to characters whose emotional state is far from the resolute grandeur of the motionless hero. Although David succeeded perfectly in balancing his picture, we can see that he had to reconcile two imperatives: that of line, which is bound to the requirements of thought, and that of color and the chromatic substance of objects, which are bound up with the impulses of feeling.

David moves us by introducing the corpse. Although funeral scenes had been frequent in eighteenth-century painting, death now seemed to appear in a new light and to be looked at with new feeling. One school, which might be described as Alexandrian and feminine, contrives to depict a nebulous and flowing sort of death, a merging amid the elements and the currents of the cosmos: Typical examples include the drowning of Virginie (painted by Vernet in 1789 and by Prud'hon later) and, in literature, Chénier's *Jeune Tarentine*, together with several graceful English representations of the death of Ophelia. But there was also a heroic, masculine school offering a proliferation of athletic corpses whose great beauty lent death an ambiguous attraction. (An aura of necrophilia hangs over all the work of David and Fuseli.) More ostensibly, the beauty of the dead was an indictment of the unfathomable injustice of Fate, while leading the onlooker's thoughts to the higher goal for which the heroes sacrificed their lives. The motionless body still lay on the edge of the material world; its living will had borne it to an intelligible ideal. The real object was revealed through a sort of play of mirrors. The spirit of the hero has attained the eternal fame for which he strove. The eye of the beholder is confronted only by the inessential, the mortal remains, but these bask in the reflected light of eternity and are depicted in terms of "ideal beauty." What matters is the heroic deed; but the dead body is transfigured by it. The age of great funeral marches—Gossec, Beethoven, and others—was not far off.

In the *Brutus* the death in question has been inflicted by the subject himself. In the paintings devoted to the martyrs of the Revolution, the theme was a death accepted and overcome in advance. By the primal act of taking the oath, the individual had agreed to die to his own personal life: He had subjected himself to a finality which fulfilled the essence of man—liberty—but at the cost of the inessential, of all that is not liberty; in other words, death. The portraits of the revolutionary martyrs show them at rest in a death which authenticates their oath as free men. By dying they have made freedom safe; they have fulfilled it. The painter's job was to present liberty as the glorious obverse of such a death. In David's *Death of Marat* (frontis.), the narrative interest, which took up so much room in the Roman pictures, is concentrated: Marat still holds Charlotte Corday's letter, and in it one can see the date (in the old style, July 13, 1793), the name of the murderess, the address ("To Citizen Marat"), and the insidious appeal, "The fact that I am most unhappy admits me to your kindness." On the packing case beside the bath is an *assignat*, or promissory note, a covering note by Marat: It reads, "Give this *assignat* to your mother. . . ." This evidence of Marat's kindness contrasts with the blood-stained kitchen knife lying on the floor. But our reading of the picture necessarily begins with the dedicatory inscription, outdoing in force the address on the letter: It runs, "To MARAT, DAVID, the year two," and is written on the bare upright of the packing case. While the letter, the answer, the *assignat*, and the knife are the clues and remains of a sudden tragedy, this inscription—a terse text in which the painter's surname, scarcely diminished by being in smaller characters, is placed in fraternal symmetry with that of the political hero—raises the death scene to the dimensions of an eternal monument. The inscription, in Roman capitals, counters, like a funeral stela, the cursive writing and the objects which bear witness to the headlong moments of the murder; it introduces a glory immune from time. The beholder finds himself pondering on the interval that separates the two moments of writing, that of Charlotte Corday writing her letter and that of David solemnly setting down his signature: That interval is filled by death and by the travail of art. We can still see the murdered Marat, but we can see him only between the two texts: We see him cease to be the man to whom Charlotte Corday gave her note on July 13, 1793, and become the man whose dead body David immortalized in year II of the Republic. Between those two dates, time was overthrown; it entered a new era and was counted from a different beginning. Baudelaire brilliantly caught this tension between the real and the ideal:

The tragedy is here, alive in all its dreadful horror, yet by a strange *tour de force* that makes this picture David's masterpiece and one of the great curiosities of modern art, there is nothing trivial or base about it. The most astonishing thing about this unusual poem is that it was painted extremely fast, which is amazing when one comes to consider the beauty of the design. It is food to the strong and the triumph of spirituality; this painting, cruel as nature, has the aura of the ideal. Where is the ugliness that holy Death has so soon wiped away with the tip of its wing? Henceforth, Marat can challenge Apollo, for Death has just brushed him with her amorous lips, and he lies in the peace of his metamorphosis. There is something at once tender and poignant in this work; through the cold air of the room, on its cold walls and around that cold and fatal bath, there moves a soul.[6]

Here again, as in the *Brutus* (which Baudelaire found "melodramatic" and did not like so much), color is so to speak driven out and restricted to the parts of the picture where the ideal is absent: It is most intense in accessories such as the green rug covering the board laid across the bath, the bare packing case, and the gray wall with its subtly modulated lights. But plastic values, drawing, predominate in the representation of the transfigured hero. To use Baudelaire's expression, drawing is here the agent of "spirituality." The tension between drawing and color is amazingly effective; contradictory postulates are balanced with supreme art. The presence of things and the dimension of thought severely coexist. To achieve this, David had to be a born colorist, fascinated first by Boucher's pinks and blues, then by Valentin's shadows; thereafter his love of pure line was the result of a slow ascesis, prescribed by his teachers to begin with and later fully accepted, in Rome, in the presence of the antique and of Domenichino, Michelangelo, and Raphael.

Even after the overcautious Pompeo Batoni named him his successor, David's pictorial temperament might still have fulfilled itself with the same chromatic liberty as Géricault or Delacroix had he not compelled himself to accept the tyranny of principle and "harsh idea." The unfinished *Bara* in the Musée Calvet in Avignon, with its glowing gold background and sweeping brush strokes, shows the freedom David was capable of in this sphere (fig. 41). The picture follows the same austere design as the *Marat* with its closed space behind the body, but here the background is radiant with color; "costume" effects are entirely eschewed and the naked subject lies dying in a luminous void: Glory is the warm brilliance created by the painting. The boy, who clutches the tricolor cockade to his heart, is an ephebe in the antique style, almost an Endymion or an Antinous. Here again line is linked to the heroic idea, to the glorious absence of issue which imprisons whosoever has taken the oath and kept his word to the end. The complete closure of linear outline is the expression

41) Jacques-Louis David (1748–1825). *Joseph Bara.* 1794.
(Avignon, Musée Calvet. Photo Musées Nationaux)

of an unflagging will (that of the painter and, by analogy, that of the character): Line, which determines things, is a symbol of moral determination. But line has a memory and refers to celebrated prototypes. The *Horatii*, which David said owed more to Poussin than to Corneille, can also be read as a bas-relief; in the *Marat*, people have detected echoes of Mantegna. Devotion to Poussin, here, means fidelity to classical tragedy and its conventions. And while, as we have seen, the oath compels him who takes it to play a preexisting role, so too line refers back to an earlier aesthetic universe: It encloses the present in the language of nostalgia. The present it encloses flees toward a past: The object depicted, anchored in the present by figurative energy, carries within it the echo of a supreme representation carried out once and for all by the ancients or by the great Italians. It figures forth an event, but the function of representation is paralleled by a dimension of reminiscence. To express the hero's fidelity to his oath, the painter finds he has to manifest his own fidelity to aesthetic standards. This was the intention of poets like Marie-Joseph Chénier, who tried to give the Revolution its own drama. In it, the rigor of Racinian tragedy was strictly imitated with great care taken over correct versification. Only the subject was topical, as in *Charles IX*, which at the end of 1789, for the first time in the French theater, showed a king of France as a criminal. It was a strange survival, which made use of rationalist arguments: Its proponents refused to see that such tragedy was doomed to mere repetition. In drama as in painting the Revolution wanted imagination to be checked and guided by reason, and reason found support in forms it rediscovered in a period before the distortions and languors, the scatterings and whittlings down, of the parodies so lavishly produced by the spirit of rococo. People wanted consciously to live through a second Renaissance better illuminated by history.[7] The artist, and above all the painter, must be able to think: David said

42)   JACQUES-LOUIS DAVID (1748–1825). *Portrait of His Jailer.*
(Rouen, Musée des Beaux Arts)

this over and over again, and so did Fuseli and Goethe. And thinking meant not only composing a picture, setting before the beholder representations of exemplary deeds, but also reinforcing the exemplarity of the subject by executing it in a style that followed an exemplary model. In a painter like David, as we have seen, the pictorial temperament and the sense of human presence, both so evident in his wonderful portraits (fig. 42), combine with another aim, which is discursive, civic, and moralistic.[8] Despite some false notes in certain of his large historical canvases, despite the rhetoric and melodrama he sometimes indulged in, he was at his best, almost in spite of himself, as a painter of the sacred, of dread, able to make the visible most intensely present just when he was subjecting it to the domination of an implacable absolute. *The Death of Marat*, a "Jacobin pietà," is a magnificent statement of the solitude of death, transmuted into communion through the universal imperative of Terror and Virtue.[9]

JOHANN

HEINRICH

FÜSSLI

(FUSELI)

43) Sir Joshua Reynolds (1723–1792). *The Death of Dido.* 1789.
(London, St. James's Palace.
Copyright Reserved. Photo A. C. Cooper)

I F THERE is an English artist who can be compared with David, it is not the charming Reynolds, who painted his last historical picture, *The Death of Dido* (fig. 43), in 1789,[1] nor the skillful and correct Benjamin West, one of the first to depict the exploits of modern arms;[2] it is rather Romney, who would have liked to paint heroic scenes taken from the loftiest poetry, but who was above all the heir of Reynolds and Gainsborough in the genre of poetic portraiture. This genre, in which the faces were enveloped in a subtle atmosphere of nobility, charm, and melancholy, was less austere and more femininely pleasing than the kind of portrait David painted, yet it could invest childish or virginal innocence with a tinge of perverse attraction. But David's real contemporary, the painter full of echoes of Homer and Rousseau, the man who gave free rein to the passion of the age, was Johann Heinrich Füssli. He was born in Zurich in 1741, and was thus seven years older than David. Between 1770 and 1780 both of them sought instruction in Rome. There David studied Valentin de Boullogne, the Carracci, Guercino, Guido, Caravaggio, and Poussin; he rethought the problems of composition and tried to reconcile line, light, and color. Füssli, whose name was modified to Fuseli to accommodate Italian speakers and who became more widely known by that version of his name in England and America, was first and foremost a draughtsman; for him, color was secondary. The only artist who mattered, for him, was Michelangelo, just because of the strength and imaginative grandeur of his draughtsmanship. He soon made up his mind which side he was on in the ancient quarrel between color and *disegno*: What interested him was the dramatic universe of human acts, not the world of matter and substance and the play of light. Though the comparison was made in their own day, it would be pointless for us to contrast Fuseli and David as Northern and Latin geniuses, respectively. Admittedly, Fuseli had a profound admiration for Shakespeare, Milton, and the Nibelungen. But his distinguishing characteristic is the way he makes the pictorial image a continuation of the literary one. David painted dramatic scenes, whereas Fuseli, even when inspired by playwrights and even when depicting actors or dancers, elaborated visions, epic scenes set in a dimension at once narrative and mental. He did away with the horizontal scenic floor upon which, in David, everything rises up in a rational manner. Drawing and composition are no longer motionless substitutes for a theatrical scene: they have no equivalent in any *tableau vivant*, and no actors could perform the parts. Vision has thrown off subjection to right angles and verisimilitude; character and beholder no longer inhabit the same space; their relationship has become at once more intimate and more strange.

David's pictures have backgrounds: The space confronting us is closed off by a wall, a colonnade, or a hanging. The characters have no means of withdrawing: They all appear to us in the foreground of a plane that reduces the depth of the stage. Fuseli's whole art rebels against this enclosure. What he postulates is a dizzying opening up of space: The beholder always

44) GEORGE ROMNEY (1734–1802). *The Tempest.*
(Rome, Galleria Nazionale d'Arte Moderna e Contemporanea)

looks upward to foreshortenings, oblique perspectives, falls and flights that make it seem as if the universe has had added to it a thousand new airy paths. While David, with his "frieze," or bas-relief, compositions, his strict antitheses and contrasted groups, breaks with the baroque system of perspective, Fuseli, aiming at fuller expressiveness, adopts the pictorial language of the Sistine Chapel and Giulio Romano. He too in his own way wanted to regenerate his art and rediscover lost grandeur: He saw himself neither as an innovator nor as a modern. In Rome he tried to find an invariable criterion of epic sublimity: He found it. Fuseli's theoretical writings show the same respect for the norms and great examples of the Renaissance as do the *Discourses* of Reynolds: He shows no inclination to plead the cause of rebellious "romanticism." It was in the name of an entirely classical doctrine that Fuseli produced a body of work that impresses us first and foremost by its strangeness.

It might be thought that he betrayed the ideal he professed. But some of the corollaries arising out of that ideal lent themselves to all kinds of distortion and farfetched application, and Fuseli made the most of them. His writings persistently claim the artist's right to expression and character. He adamantly resisted Winckelmann's theory, so attractive to some, according to which serenity, calm, and impassivity were the necessary conditions of true beauty, and signs of passion were inferior and in conflict with harmony of line. In Fuseli's view this was a misunderstanding of the higher essence of Greek art, in which he saw emotional intensity and the requirements of form as closely interlinked.

The example of the Greeks and of Michelangelo licensed him to pursue the highest possible degree of expressive energy, on the one condition that it did not jeopardize the clarity and elegance of monumental form. Art might make use of great terrors, but it should stop short where horror begins: Dread must remain pure, distinct from disgust and repulsion. In this way nobility of style would be preserved, together with the alliance between emotional expressiveness and the spiritual principle, mind.

In fact, this search for emotional expressiveness was to revive not Michelangelo himself but the mannerist school to which he gave rise. Fuseli's imagination tended toward the superlative, and his version of the heroic image portrayed an athletic physique in the most violent action. The action covers an enormous space, and the masculine figure is always seen at the culminating point of his exploit. What is expressed by these bodies at the climax of effort is crime and sin. Fuseli's female figures, on the other hand, are excessively feminine. They are lengthened and drawn out; they seem to soar, or sink into a mortal languor. They are creatures of dream, and dream gives them sometimes the slim grace of an elf, sometimes the giant stature of a goddess. They are either supernaturally light or supernaturally heavy. Thus here, from the outset, the desire for expression brings about a metamorphosis of bodies in accordance with the energy or languor with which they are filled. In Fuseli, expression and character manifest themselves in exaggerated gesture before becoming action: We witness a dreamed crisis set in the imaginary space of the drawing, not on the earth of common reality. In Fuseli's work the exaggeration is the result of a complete break with the conventions of literal resemblance. What he drew and painted was a plastic transposition of the feeling of intensity aroused by reading the great works of literature. In this sense he was indeed the continuator of historical painting (like David and his followers, he had only contempt for genre painting); but he put into it all the liberties of the art of illustration. Concerned as he was with psychological effect, and himself caught up in a reverie which obstinately repeated its obsessional motifs, he had no time for the accuracy of "costume," which weighed down historical painting. He did not, like David, turn to archaeology for the shape of the chairs the Romans sat in. Fuseli dressed or undressed his characters as he pleased, sometimes listening to the suggestions of fashion, and he transposed antique drama into a setting that might have been designed by Soane or Adam.

Fuseli looked to literature for the essential motive force. Pencil in hand, he acted the text to himself, elaborating in bold lines the hitherto intangible witness to the epic or dramatic word. Like Delacroix later, he subjected himself at his own risk to the law of poetry. From 1786 on he worked enthusiastically for Boydell's Shakespeare Gallery; his great amibition after 1790 was a Milton Gallery, executed by himself alone and not completed until 1800.

Lessing, in his *Laocoön*, had attributed action (*Handlung*) to literature, and calm power (*ruhende Gestaltung*) to the fine arts; literature's sphere was the successive, art's the simultaneous. Fuseli, in his scenes inspired by the tragic poets and the great epics, made the fullest use of poetic action, setting down violent moments of such action or other moments, often terrible ones, when it was imminent. A kind of narrative impatience made him tend to avoid simultaneity and give his figures the boundless mobility of literary images. The dramatic effect seems to spread from the moment in question out into all directions in time. We have a presentiment of a past and a future, and they are usually terrifying. The scene we see is lit up by brimstone between two instants of darkness.

So all Fuseli's work was of the imagination, even his rare portraits. There is no use looking in Fuseli for the naturalist's accuracy which, in Stubbs, produces strangeness through its very meticulousness and patient attention to detail. Stubbs's marvelous painting *The Phaeton* shows a carriage surrounded by lush vegetation too paradisial not to portend sin and woe, and ready to drive us off into the realms of the novel (fig. 45). Fuseli disdained such recourse to realism, as he also disdained the veracity and down-to-earth fidelity of Gainsborough, who died in 1788 and whose chief works were shown in a big exhibition the following year. He was not the chronicler of high society, like Raeburn and Romney; he lacked the colorist's skill and the faculty of flattering docility vis-à-vis the model. He left "distinguished portraiture" to Lawrence, who was twenty years old in 1789 and an immediate success in high society (by 1792, when he was twenty-three, he was painter to the king). For Fuseli could not breathe easily until he was up in the lofty regions of the great tragic fables in which human destiny is torn between good and evil. The drama which the French Revolution introduced into contemporary history was seen by Fuseli in his own way, as a legend and in terms of its imaginative dimension. As an ardent reader of Rousseau, he believed that evil increased in proportion to the progress of civilization. Like Goya, he wanted to defend the ideal of enlightenment, but when he confronted the adversary he expressed its power by means of massive symbols. He was fascinated by the workings of the evil he thus tried to exorcize, and hailed the beauty of Milton's Satan. While his *Nightmare* (1782) may have been intended partly as an allegorical denunciation of the uneasiness hanging over England, its main purpose was to depict the mortal ecstasy of a tortured sleeper: The strange pleasure we take in this scene of terror contrives, insidiously, to make us the accomplices of evil. Such are the marvelous dangers of an art which is inspired by a great moral purpose but which insists on taking account of all the dark regions of the world of the mind: Perhaps Fuseli lingered there longer than he should. A kind of mad strength made its appearance, a spell was cast that encroached on the original intention of the artist's everyday consciousness. Fuseli loses his way among the nocturnal regions of a land of cruelty, comparable to that invented by Sade, over which there hovers a dreadful doom. It is peopled by languorous victims, half-clad in long, transparent draperies, but also by cruel woman in her various forms: proud Valkyries and courtesans who might be lewd empresses, with naked bosoms and hair piled up into elaborate coiffures like wrought silver. Woman, a victim in some of Fuseli's visions, here becomes a perverse and solemn executioner, surrounded by a strange

45) GEORGE STUBBS (1724–1806). *The Phaeton.*
(London, National Gallery)

luxury that is a distorted reflection of the Oriental riches of Georgian England.

In this way Fuseli's art built up a bizarre and sensuous universe in which unbridled imagination, reminiscences of Michelangelo, and classical, Germanic, and medieval themes combined in order to illustrate Shakespeare or Milton, Ariosto or Wieland. Not the least of the charms of this art is its absolute anachronism. Its exemplary value lies in its unstable mixture of the voluntary and the involuntary, of emotional energy (allied to that of *Sturm und Drang*) and cold curiosity about evil. Fuseli's work, which was inspired by literature and greatly admired by certain writers, bears an astonishing resemblance to the dark, fantastic creations of authors like Beckford, Lewis, and Ann Radcliffe— though Fuseli did not rate these novelists very highly. He wanted to be an epic painter, not an artist of dream. His writings contain only a passing reference in favor of dream, which shows that, in his work, dream is not something deliberate but something arising out of an inner necessity despite a vigilance that believed itself stronger than dream.

Here we come upon one of the characteristic features of the late eighteenth century. Reason, conscious of its powers, sure of its prerogatives, welcomed the forces of feeling and passion and looked to them as sources of additional energy. In this way it thought to unify man in the light of good and intellect. It thought it could turn everything into light. But, once having granted desire all its rights, reason found it had acquired elements of darkness and dream that it had hitherto excluded. The dividing line between day and

46)   JOHANN HEINRICH FÜSSLI (1741–1825). *Three Courtesans*.
1799–1800. (Kunstmuseum Basel)

night became an inner frontier, and thought soon became the subject of prolonged interrogation. Art was no longer the work of a will that was perfectly clear and lucid; in a consciousness that had been extended to include a whole element of darkness, art became an adventurous quest that plunged into shadow in search of images whose strange shapes, seen in the light of day, would bear the indelible stigmata of thier origin.

An artist who refuses to imitate nature in all the detail of its particularities and who clings to the vast generality of tragic fable is bound nevertheless to confront us with another kind of particularity—that of the individual and of his personal dreams and torments. Such an art develops in a dimension of subjective idealism, inventing a separate world, a mental spectacle, against a background of darkness. Goethe, spokesman of classical reason, mistrusted it, only to construct instead, to exorcize his own shades, a pandemonium that has something in common with that of Fuseli. Conversely, other artists, under the influence of Winckelmann and with the theoretical patronage of Goethe, were to experiment in everyday idealism. But a careful observer will see several points of contact between the impetuous and incomplete art of Fuseli on the one hand and radical neoclassicism on the other: They intersect in a no-man's-land between night and day, in a cold crepuscular or lunar light, in a place where light is dimmed, and instead of fixing what it illuminates, becomes amorous caress and cool tenderness. The meeting takes place under the aegis of Endymion.

ROME

AND

NEOCLASSICISM

47) ANNE-LOUIS GIRODET (1767–1824). *Endymion.*
(Paris, Musée du Louvre. Photo Musées Nationaux)

W HILE ROCOCO was dying in a melancholy and ironic twilight in Venice, 1789 saw the working out in Rome of an artistic doctrine and practice destined to culminate in what would be called the "Empire" style. In fact, it was a European style that spread in England, Germany, and Italy as well as in France.

Rome, in the year 1789, was more cosmopolitan than ever. The first French émigrés could be met with there: the king's aunts and their entourage; Madame Vigée-Lebrun; and they were welcomed by France's representative, Cardinal de Bernis, who was as well a writer of light verse. Also in Rome were some young French artists sympathetic to the Revolution; these were closely watched by the papal police, who pursued them for their Masonic connections. Percier and Fontaine, later to be architects and decorators to Napoleon, were in Rome too in 1789. Percier had been commissioned by the Academy to make a study of Trajan's Column. Together with Fontaine he acquired a repertoire of motifs in Naples and Pompeii, where he formed his decorative vocabulary and included in it many "Etruscan" elements. Chinard, the sculptor, left Rome in 1789 but returned in 1791. Quatremère de Quincy had just completed a long visit, which he recalled in his *Dictionnaire d'Architecture*, his biography of Canova, and his studies on Raphael. Flaxman, after a long collaboration with Wedgwood, arrived in Italy in 1787. In Rome he found a group of Englishmen whose leading light was Gavin Hamilton. He probably met Gagnereaux, who practiced line drawing. Canova was working on his *Psyche* and on the *Mausoleum of Clement XIII*. Angelika Kaufmann reigned over her salon; Goethe, whose portrait she had painted, had just gone back to Germany. Wilhelm Tischbein, after living in Rome for many years, settled in Naples. Girodet, who won the Grand Prix in 1789, arrived in Rome at the beginning of 1790: It was there that he painted his *Endymion* (fig. 47) and his *Hippocrates Refusing the gifts of Artaxerxes*. Carstens, a latecomer, appeared in Roman artistic circles in 1792.

These artists and theoreticians were passionate readers of Winckelmann and Mengs. Their enthusiasm was reinforced by an idea: They were returning to the antique—to Greek sculpture, to the drawings on classical vases, to Roman architecture—and to Mantegna, Raphael, Michelangelo, and Correggio; but for them this return was not a whim of taste, an impulsive preference. It was a decision founded on reason, a premeditated choice. After a century which seemed to them to have been characterized by a chaotic exaltation of emotional values and superficial joys, their chosen mission was to bring art back under the authority of thought. They no longer saw the dramatic richness of baroque or the subtle prodigalities of rococo as marks of mind but only as stimulants of a dubious pleasure from which soul was absent. They therefore wanted to do away with the deadly seductions of "manner" and affectation, which in their view represented only a loss of force. And to restore simplicity and strength, to free the captive soul from excessive finery, they appealed to nature, to the ideal, to the art of the days when European

civilization was young. They tried to recover possession of a truth from which, in their view, baroque and
rococo had separated them by a forest of illusions. They
wanted to escape from the garden of Armida.[1] But
would they indeed be cured of the depressing lassitude
to which so many late eighteenth-century writers bear
witness? We have to admit that not all of them were
able to draw on new sources of energy. For many of
them this path, instead of leading to a second Renaissance, was only to end in an art that was impoverished,
dim, and bloodless. But the others, even though their
style was nourished by a borrowed light and heat,
merit attention for their intentions as well as their suc-
cesses.

If we consider their quest, we see that the great idea
of a beginning, or a beginning again, a regeneration,
which was manifested in history by the Revolution,
was far from being applied in the sphere of political
institutions alone. Goethe, throughout his journey to
Italy, continually meditated upon the "original plant"
and the primal principle governing the organization of
the vegetable kingdom. In their own sphere, the artists
he met in Rome also tried to draw near the light that
shone in the beginning. They felt they were participat-
ing in a revolution that was also a resurrection: Quatremère de Quincy formulated the task as that of
"rekindling the torch of antiquity."[2]

If they appealed to nature, it was first and foremost
to its original intentions, before the deviations and ec-
centricities imposed by the resistance of matter. And if
they imitated the sculpture and drawing of the Greeks,
it was because the latter, drawing freely from the source

itself, and untroubled and uncorrupted by the sight of any factitious models, spoke innocently and faithfully the language of nature.

The moderns were bound to try to forget the methods they had learned, in order to let themselves be ruled by the antique vigor. They had to rediscover truth, either by immediately abandoning themselves to the impetus of genius or by studying the works in which genius had manifested itself. The appeal was at once to the freest spontaneity and to the most vigilant reflection. The artist wanted to be without a memory, but he listened to Homer and looked at the *Laocoön*.

The advent of the light, which the revolutionary spirit tried to bring about by founding the new Republic, was experienced by these artists as an upsurge at once topical and immemorial. As we know, the idea of a primal revelation found various expressions during the eighteenth century, sometimes going back to the biblical image of Adam talking with God, sometimes in the form of theosophical or other unorthodox variations. The first man and the first nations received the whole of art and of knowledge, and history had only dimmed the meaning of that first illumination. Rabaut Saint-Etienne, following the teaching of both Bailly and Court de Gébelin, regarded the Greek myths themselves as a degenerate version of an original allegorical "scripture." How could one bask in the original light except by that act which makes us its symbolic contemporary—that is, by initiation? The historian of ideas would find an extensive field for research in the Platonic and Neoplatonic revival that occurred around 1789 in almost all the countries of Europe: In England, where Blake was influenced by the "orphic" writings and translations of Thomas Taylor; in Holland, where Hemsterhuis wrote dialogues in the manner of Plato; in France, where in 1790 Joubert put forward the idea of "traveling in those open spaces where one can see nothing but light . . . like Plato";[3] and in Germany, where Hegel, Hölderlin, and Schelling, pupils at the seminary at Tübingen, read Plato, Proclus, and Iamblichus when their enthusiasm for the French Revolution was at its height. A thirst for an intelligible Beauty, a reflection of the unity of Being, emerged strongly everywhere—in reaction, as we have seen, against the corrupting seduction of sensual pleasure. People aspired to an art that would no longer address itself to the eyes alone, but instead, though through the inevitable mediation of sight, to the soul. For a number of years the myth of Psyche was widely invoked, not only to express a profounder sensibility to everything concerning love but much more because the art that aimed at reaching the soul felt a need to represent itself by means of allegory and emblem. In fact, if the goal was really the ideal in the metaphysical sense of the term, the work itself could only be seen as an emblem of an unattainable reality: Art, the language of the senses, could never be anything but an allegory, or *analogon*, of the suprasensible. We may recall that allegory made a remarkable return to favor at the end of the eighteenth century, comparable to the way it flourished in the sixteenth century under the influence of Ficino and Pico della Mirandola. But in a world where the acceptable way of thinking of things had been profoundly modified by mathematical physics, the image no longer had the quasi-magical function it had in the Renaissance, with its cosmos peopled by spiritual correlations and crossed by the fields of force of sympathy and "correspondences." The allegorical image now found itself, so to speak, confronted by a dilemma, a choice between meaning by remote control, on the one hand, and the more mysterious participation, on the other. Meaning by remote control, as one might guess, consisted of treating the essential nature of forms as a system of signs that were to disappear and be replaced by their own intellectual explanation. That being so, the image disappeared, giving way to the discourse of which it was the visual equivalent. Image served sense but was abandoned as a mere intermediary whose beauty was beside the point as soon as its meaning had been arrived at by the reason of the beholder. Participation, on the other hand, more faithful to the spirit of Platonism, links image indissolubly to idea: Image presents itself to us not as a distant and separate sign of a thought but as the presence of the absolute in the world of the senses. (In the same way, we have seen the revolutionary emblem arise at the point where the light of principle encountered everyday reality.) When idea participates fully in image, when the one is irrevocably inherent in the other, an infinite suspense enters into artistic discourse and mysteriously offers to stand for all discourse: We must speak no longer of allegory but of symbol. As Goethe hoped, "Allegory transforms appearance into concept, and concept into image, but in such a way that the concept in the image remains definite, can be fully understood and grasped, and can therefore be stated. Symbolism transforms appearance

48) Bénigne Gagnereaux (1756–1795). *The Wheel of Ixion*.
(Stockholm, Nationalmuseum)

into idea, and idea into image, but in such a way that the idea in the image remains eternally active and out of reach; and even if it were expounded in every language it would remain inexpressible."[4] A symbolic idea acts as an intermediary between appearance and image, but in such a way that in the image it lives on forever.

Image, made subject to the requirements of idea, was to expel all alien matter. It would try to throw off all that was no more than sensual superfluity. It would strip away all that imprisoned it in bodily contingency. Engraving and line drawing, as practiced by Gagnereaux, Flaxman, and Carstens (most of them men from the North!), found their aesthetic justification in the graphic style of the Greek vases: What these artists were doing was returning to a primal kind of drawing, a calligraphy that was infallible, an art that belonged to the beginning.[5] But this justification, based on history and on the archaeological attraction of objects miraculously saved from time and the soil, was reinforced by profounder considerations concerning the nature of the soul. "The soul," wrote Hemsterhuis, "judges most beautiful that of which it can form an idea in the briefest space of time. . . . It likes to have a great number of ideas in the smallest space of time possible."[6] It is through line, and the greatest possible simplicity of drawing compatible with the subjects represented, that the soul can enjoy this pleasure: "We distinguish visible objects by the lines they present to us, by the way their configuration modifies shadows and light, and lastly by their color: One might say that it is *solely by their lines*, since color is only a secondary quality, and since modification of light and shade is only the result of a profile

49) ASMUS JAKOB CARSTENS (1754–1798). *Self-Portrait.*
(Hamburg Kunsthalle)

50) JOSIAH WEDGWOOD (1730–1795).
Vase with an apotheosis of Homer by John Flaxman (1755–1826).
(Nottingham Castle Museum, England. Photo Layland-Ross)

which we do not see." For Hemsterhuis all art consisted in the concentration of ideas into forms that could be deciphered in the minimum of time: "It seems beyond dispute that there is something in our souls which dislikes having anything to do with what we call succession and duration." Hemsterhuis believed that sculpture was invented before drawing and painting[7]—but this was so that the two latter might derive from sculpture, or rather from the intermediary genre of bas-relief. "This abstract idea of line was absolutely necessary to bring to birth drawing and painting."[8]

David had already offered a fine example of linearity, a reminiscence of bas-relief. But strong shadows and intense colors were also to be found in his work. They gave the rational energy that controlled them a chance to manifest itself; they bore witness to the strict determination that tamed and disciplined them. From drawing and the minor genre of line engraving, shade and color were expelled and tension abolished. A single principle reigned without opposition. By means of form and line, the mind labored to fix the ideal type. It was a labor that claimed to echo the intentions of nature, but in fact it owed less to direct contemplation of reality than to the interposition of those who had grasped it and fixed it earlier. It was not really nature in its immediacy that these artists loved but the beautiful earlier forms in which they saw the art of the ancients harmoniously bring to perfection what nature itself had only sketched. Paradigm interposed all the time between the world and them. A golden age of art had been lost, and they could not forget it. And so, in their practice of drawing, so greatly oriented and

[151]

guided by the memory of Greek draughtsmanship, they imprisoned themselves in myth. Flaxman illustrated the *Iliad* and the *Odyssey* and Aeschylus; Carstens would only deal with antique or heroic subjects, and his last composition, in 1797, was a *Golden Age*. Art exiled itself in a past already illuminated by art and sought refuge in the universe of the poets. Neoclassicism (or, if you like, hyperclassicism) was based on a great absence: Line determined forms which were at once swallowed up again in the light of the past.

But to this idealism presupposing the supremacy of an absolute external model (seen as intention in nature and as perfection in human art) were added the justifications of another idealism that was entirely subjective. A stroke in a drawing was the act of a free mind under no obligation to imitate: According to Fernow, Carstens not only did not copy but also refused to reproduce anything from memory. What was at work in his compositions was "the plastic power of his imagination."[9] And so, as in David, linearity corresponds to the exercise of the artist's will: The formal "determination" that results in line bears witness to the supremacy of the creative consciousness. For both Fernow and Carstens the primacy of the creative act had a corollary in a refusal to subject art to the dogmas of the Christian religion. Once "ideal liberty" had been discovered, the artist would find in art his true religion, "that is, the object of his purest love."[10]

To compare once more this aspect of neoclassical art with the characteristic features of rococo, I prefer to leave aside the fluttering lights and shades and the complicated ornament and turn instead to a minor aspect of rococo, silhouette, which strikes me as the complete antithesis of line engraving. Silhouette presents itself as the passively projected shadow of a real person in his or her daily attire and accustomed gestures; it is the tracing of a profile. All that the silhouettist tries to do is follow as skillfully as possible the edges of an image thrown on the glass of the camera obscura; nothing of himself is involved. Line drawing, on the other hand, reflects the autonomy of a consciousness that presides over every moment during which the hand moves over the page. This trajectory was often too stiff and cautious in an artist like Flaxman, despite his heroic aspirations. In Carstens it unfolded in a sort of hypnotic calm. The danger besetting this kind of art, if it followed too closely the injunctions of Winckelmann (for whom beauty, "insipid" and neutral as pure water, had to blossom in the impassive calm of serene form), was lethargy—elusive fluidity or deadly petrification. Consciousness, in complete control, ran the risk of falling in love, like Narcissus, with its own purity and of coming to a standstill in an unsubstantial dream of transparency.

The salvation of this art, one might guess, could have lain in a return to darkness, to what, to use Freudian terminology, had been repressed. But this hyperclassical art first included a new type of darkness in its subjects, while its technique remained unchanged. Thus in Flaxman the calm ideality of the forms was disturbed by the expressive intensity of the violence, the heroic fury, the terror and dread that they depicted. A semiabstract ballet, later to influence Picasso, arose out of the need to combine movement with

51)   ASMUS JAKOB CARSTENS (1754–1798).
Night with Her Children Sleep and Death. 1795.
(Kunstsammlungen zu Weimar—DDR)

an evocation of the torments of the soul. We should not forget that, significantly enough, Flaxman's work as a line draughtsman came between providing decorations for Wedgwood and carrying out commissions for memorial sculptures—in other words, between elegant adventitiousness and an art devoted to immortalizing grief and consolation. And although Carstens imparted an atmosphere of great quiet into his works, he also introduced an inner dimension by virtue of which the characters, nearly all of them motionless, are nevertheless animated by a mental drama. As Rudolf Zeitler has perceptively remarked, Carstens often contrasts active characters (Homer or Orpheus chanting, Priam beseeching) with meditative onlookers; and just as he can suggest the dimension of thought, so also he can convey a sense of depth in time. His solemn figures seem to be withdrawn into consciousness of themselves, that is, of inner time. This mental perspective is not just some neutral, empty "cogito"; behind those eyes apparently blind to the real world is a dim sense of destiny. One of Carstens's major works—inspired by Hesiod— was *Night and Her Children* (fig. 51): in other words, the mythical origin of fate.

CANOVA

AND THE

ABSENT

GODS

52)   ANTONIO CANOVA (1757–1822). *Criton Closing the Eyes of Socrates.*
(Possagno, Treviso, Gipsoteca Canoviana)

S UBTLY BUT surely the work of Canova too was influenced by the return of darkness. Admittedly, smoothness and polish, calm and hypnotic coolness seem to predominate in many of his sculptures: In his work, the principle of linearity developed through the medium of bright, sleek surfaces. But Canova, like David, came to the neoclassical ideal from another direction. In both, up to a point, the demands of a public of connoisseurs carried weight. When Canova arrived in Rome in 1779, with the *Daedalus and Icarus* he had executed in Venice, he was criticized and advised by a group of artists and art lovers who had read Winckelmann and were familiar with the collections in the Vatican. (It would be difficult to exaggerate the importance of the Vatican Museum in the rise of the neoclassical style; Pope Clement XIV had made its antique statuary available to the public in 1773.) What was wrong, then, with Canova's *Daedalus and Icarus?* According to Quatremère de Quincy, it limited itself to the sort of "identical imitation" that "merely attempts a kind of reproduction of the individual"—a "banal and vulgar" imitation that remains the captive of the particular and "addresses itself only through what might be called a material reality to a limited comprehension."[1] Canova was even suspected of having molded his figures from living bodies. What his critics aimed at was leading this gifted young artist toward the revival of the antique—a revival that avoided slavish copying. He needed to turn away from "identical" imitation and discover the secret of "ideal" imitation; instead of taking a "live model" for nature, he must take nature itself for a model. Quatremère de Quincy claimed to have told Canova that in ideal imitation "the mind can use the parallel of individuals to produce an idea of perfection and beauty the image of which nature may never have taken the trouble to complete. It belongs to art alone to provide the necessary supplement, because art has but one goal while nature has thousands."[2] The *Theseus* which Canova executed in Rome between 1781 and 1782 was greeted by connoisseurs as "the first example provided in Rome of the revival of the style, system, and principles of antiquity."[3]

Was it an accident that these two works, separated by the transition from one style to the other, were both inspired by the legend of Daedalus? Daedalus is seen fixing a wing to Icarus' shoulder: The youth's desire for flight is suggested by his posture and by the feather he holds in his right hand. In his painting, sketches, and many of his sculptures, Canova continued to meditate on this theme: His *amorini* with their rounded wings, his spirits and his Love with ampler plumage, his leaping dancers, all fill his work with the beating of pinions and the joy of flight. The work still makes use of the contrast, beloved of baroque artists, between the raw material, stone, and the light draperies or feathers which it is made to portray and which deny the weight of the marble. On the other hand, Theseus is seated on the body of the bull-faced monster: With his club resting against the side of the vanquished beast, he meditates on the fact that the terrors of the labyrinth are behind him, the fight is over, and the enemy that ruled over the shades is now delivered over to the darkness of death. Human strength has triumphed. Canova, who chose the subject quite freely, may have wanted it to be a symbolic expression of his own victory over desire: He is not known to have had any love affairs or indulged in any passions. What is important to note is that when he was doing his best to make his art conform to the requirements of the ideal, he introduced an element of violence into it, made it skirt death, as if by an instinctive desire to counterbalance the calm and placidity which the use of pure forms might have caused to predominate. His work presents an alternation between graceful subjects and scenes of extreme fury, as in the group of *Hercules and Lichas*, inspired by *The Trachinian Women*, in which the enraged hero throws the lad who has brought him the shirt of Nessus into the sea.

But let us consider the works Canova was engaged on in 1789: the *Funeral Monument to Clement XIII*, *Love and Psyche*, and the bas-reliefs on *The Death of Socrates*. Death is omnipresent, in forms either solemn, suave, or serene. Socrates, as in David, is the personification of philosophical assurance and foreknowledge of the mysteries of death. He is ready to pass fearlessly from this world to the next.

In the mausoleum (fig. 53), Canova, as Zeitler's shrewd analyses have shown, differentiated levels and spaces in such a way as to make areas of emptiness perform a vital function.[4] The figures are independent; there is no direct relation between one and another. We are a long way here from the dynamic groups of the baroque, where all the figures contribute to one pur-

53) Antonio Canova (1757–1822). *Funeral Monument to Clement XIII.*
(Rome, St. Peter's Church. Photo Brogi-Giraudon)

pose. The pope, praying, his eyes closed, is a simulacrum of a living man; but he is deep in meditation, and
stands out against a background of nothingness that
Zeitler calls a "great empty niche." Religion, upright
and severe, rays of light springing from her brow and
holding the Cross in one hand, rests the other on the
sarcophagus. She gazes into the distance, neither at the
sky, nor at the deceased, nor at the beholder: Her sober,
watchful countenance holds no promise of ecstasy, no
foretaste of resurrection. This straight, almost stiff figure, its attitude in such strong contrast to those of the
others in the composition, is enough in itself to denote
immovable fidelity to revealed truth. Nearer to us, half-
reclining with its elbow on the base of the sarcophagus,
the spirit of death, with its torch held upside down,
seems deep in a melancholy dream. This posture of
abandonment suggests that Canova intended the figure
not so much as an emblem of death, corresponding
symmetrically to the allegory of Religion, as a representation of the very act of dying—a fluid action in which
the subject lets himself be swept away by an invisible
wave. Is this an image of Christian death? The lions at
the base of the monument recall the Venetian origins of
Pope Rezzonico: The one lying at the feet of Religion
is growling, while the other, the companion of Thana-
tos, drowses. What a distance is placed here between
the figures themselves, and what a distance between
them and us! Only the Faith is really awake, while
prayer, the sleep of death, and the drowsy lion create
an insurmountable separation, an inwardness beyond
our reach. Here shade is not only a vast system of
empty spaces behind or between the figures; it is also

[163]

the "depth" behind the closed eyes, the unseen power to which Death happily resigns itself. Shade is not present positively, but acts silently, under the surface, in the work's invisible structure.

In comparison *Love and Psyche* (fig. 54) seems at first glance a frivolous piece of work, an erotic base for a clock, at once daring and cold. Wordsworth criticized the group for its sensuality. The vigilant Quatremère could not help telling Canova that he was afraid his "extreme facility, and a sort of stylistic coquetry, might make him gradually stray from the paths of simple truth, innocence, and antique purity. . . . I remember too (as he afterward reminded me) saying he should beware of becoming an *antique Bernini*."[5] But if we study the work with the attention it deserves, if we set aside the almost abstract charm of the oblique patterns made by the bodies, arms, and wings, we see a dying creature being saved, in its last throes, by Love. As Friederike Brun has said, "Psyche is shown at the moment when she is about to succumb, enveloped in the *Stygian vapors* emanating from Proserpine's jar, which she has just opened."[6] So the female figure in the group is on the very brink of death, about to perish in the extremity of despair. But Love has descended from heaven. The moment Canova has chosen to depict is not that of an amorous embrace but that of the first contact with the divine, a contact that brings back to life a persecuted creature already caught up in the shadow of death. Darkness, in this work, is a frontier which is very near, although the scene itself is shown upon the shore of light. Psyche has just emerged from depths of darkness; she is coming alive again. As Zeit-

54)   ANTONIO CANOVA (1757–1822). *Love and Psyche*.
Venice, Museo Correr. Photo Toso)

ler has written, "The sculpted surface, which has been
treated with the utmost delicacy, makes the beholder
feel the slightest contact as charged with meaning; in
this sense, and in this sense only, can the group *Love
and Psyche* be said to possess an erotic content."[7] Experience teaches that the most intense erotic values

arise out of an ambivalence between day and night, the juxtaposition of light and darkness, a presence at once offered and withdrawn. The fingers of Venus touch the face of Adonis for the last time before the mortal chase, leaving unbroken an innocence forever safe from the contamination of the sinful world (fig. 56).

In 1788 the Abbé Barthélemy, in his *Voyage du Jeune Anacharsis*, used the story of a young Scythian's travels to show what life in Greece was like in the days of Plato. According to this account, the world of the Greeks was animated by a vague sort of romanticism, practically an ideal model for eighteenth-century society to imitate: Wisdom, friendship, good citizenship, piety, national ceremonies, tragedy—all seemed to combine in one harmonious example. If history was made up of cycles and periods (and this was one of the meanings of the ambiguous term *revolution* as it was then used), why should men not hope to live once again in that antique light and according to that eternal Norm? The book was an enormous success, and, in that age of extreme and contradictory enthusiasms, cast a spell over some of its readers. People gave "Greek banquets,"[8] and David remembered the procession of the Panathenaeans when he organized the Feast of the Supreme Being. One whole aspect of neoclassical art can be defined as an attempt to enter into the deeds, roles, and feelings exemplified in the great models: The Beautiful, as reflected in the Greek past, invited people to identify with it, urged them to revive it through their love and energy. Would not a return to the One which seemed to lie behind that primal Beauty be a way of restoring human brotherhood? Schiller's great

55) Antonio Canova (1757–1822). *Love and Psyche.*
(Paris, Musée du Louvre. Photo Musées Nationaux)

ode *Die Künstler*, published in 1789, says precisely that, using the image of white light, which brings together all the colors in the spectrum. But it also says that the truth which used to be offered to men in the guise of Beauty is now offered in the guise of Knowledge. A new power had come to birth, creating a gulf between men and the "naive" Beauty of their beginnings, yet helping them to recognize it as a foreshadowing of their own knowledge. Thus at the very moment when historical consciousness rediscovered the original light, it saw how far away it now was, and how distant the model of antique harmony.[9] To attempt, at such a juncture, to imitate the way of life of the Ancients would be to live a lie, to deny the power of distancing and reflection that was now the very essence of consciousness. The only authentic relationship with Greece and its gods was one which obliged people to accept that they were things of the past: Modern men had to resign themselves to the insuperable difference which doomed them to live their own history, to progress in a way which could no longer be based on a previous model. This brings us to the other side of neoclassical art: that which is aware of the distance separating it from the forms it represents, which knows it is aiming at a kind of absence. It turned out that poetry was better able than sculpture or painting to compute the distance and declare the impossibility of a return to the beginning, and, out of this impossibility, to create the great modern themes: the lyricism of the separate consciousness, of memory, and of the lost presence. Do we accord Canova too much honor if we see him—the last artist in the great Italian "classical" tra-

56a, b, & c)   Antonio Canova (1757–1822). *Venus and Adonis.*
(Collection Musée d'art et d'histoire, Genève)

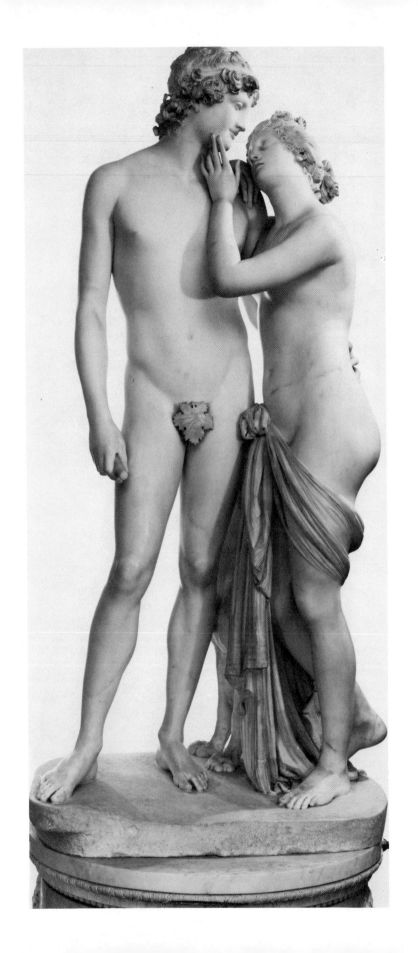

dition—as a sculptor who, despite the exactness of his lines, was able to indicate the limitation and circumscription which suggest that his creations are illusory, like nostalgic ghosts about to fade from our sight and seek refuge in a past world? His figures, seeking to escape us, hint that the artist was trying to reveal an intentionally elusive reflection of a Beauty that the Ancients themselves had made eternal.[10]

THE

RECONCILIATION

WITH

DARKNESS

G OETHE DEVOTED much thought to light and color during his visit to Italy, and when he got back to Weimar he began to experiment. His first published work on the subject, *Beiträge zur Optik*, appeared in 1791.[1] Its central idea, lying behind the whole theory, is that color is the result of the polarity between light and darkness. The principle of polarity is found in the eye itself: In effects of successive or simultaneous contrast, it produces the color complementary to that presented to it from without. "It is the eternal formula of life which is here expressed. If the eye is offered darkness it demands light; and if light is brought near it, it demands darkness. In this way it demonstrates its vitality, its right to grasp the object while at the same time producing out of its own activity something which is opposed to the object."[2] This principle of polarity linking light to darkness and subject to object applies also to the moral universe: It is the very principle of the universe.[3] Mephistopheles was to say: "I myself am a part of the part which in the beginning was all, a part of the darkness that gave birth to light, the proud light who now contends with her mother Night for her ancient rank and the space she used to occupy; but she meets with little success; for despite her efforts she can only creep over the surface of the bodies which bring her to a halt; she but runs over that surface and lends it color."[4] Here we see not only a return to darkness but darkness itself proclaimed a universal source: Light is a secondary fount, and the struggle between the two extremes produces the beauty of the world. In this cosmic confrontation, man is not merely the stake or the witness in an event outside himself. He is the field in which the encounter takes place; but he is also the medium through which a transcendence occurs. He has his own darkness within, yet his eye possesses a light akin to that of the sun. And when man looks at the world, when he contemplates and understands it, and still more when he produces something new by applying the law of style to the thing contemplated, he becomes the creator of a second nature within nature itself, where the balance doomed everywhere else to evanescence at last becomes eternal.

This belief in creative antagonism and the fertility of darkness, this recourse to polarity, is also to be found at the same period in the works of Blake. The *Songs of Innocence* (1789) and the *Songs of Experience* (1794) together represent, according to their subtitle, "the Two Contrary States of the Human Soul." The songs reflecting birth and childhood happiness and budding strength are followed by others which see youth doomed to want and fear and frustration and to all the works of evil. Man has to leave childish innocence behind and face up to evil and sin in order to enter into spiritual life and prophetic vision. *The Marriage of Heaven and Hell* (1790) heralded the end of the world and the resurrection of man in his true body, now increased to giant size. But for this to come about the world of desire (the hell of orthodox theologies) must be reconciled with the world of the spirit: The fire that burns in darkness, to which hypocritical moralities consign the damned, has to unite with the light of

Heaven. New life is born of the "diabolical" conflagration that destroys fallen existence and induces imaginative vision. Energy, condemned by moralizing reason, "is eternal delight." Halfheartedness, prudence, mistrust, the prisons built to defend the social order are the true hell, and "Opposition is true Friendship." This aphorism might be the motto of all Blake's paintings and graphic works. Everywhere in them we see opposition (which within Blake's style itself becomes the implicit opposition between the symbolizer and the symbolized), everywhere we see tension and struggle; but the conflict is resolved in the great harmonious forms of circle, vortex, and spiral. Dramatic gesture, superhuman feats of leaping and flight go far beyond the bounds of earthly reality, and the images of transgression and liberation form part of vast swirlings and ribbed surgings reflecting the way energy circulates within the cosmos. For me Blake's most striking works are not those which fill the sky with flights of angels or transform a falling body into a flaming torch: These are somewhat stereotyped reminders of the Michelangelo model as transmitted and reworked by Fuseli. Blake affects one more deeply when in contrast with such figures he depicts huge, ill-proportioned, primitively wild beings with great bestial countenances reflecting the inertia and melancholy of the earth, impenetrable darkness, and chthonic heaviness; all this in a universe where air, water, and fire are filled with waves of ethereal beings. Earth is dark, night threatens; the air is unbreathable, and life can be nothing but a long ordeal—unless its bounds are broken through and a universe of light opened up to our freed imagination. Apocalypse is the only revolution Blake can conceive of. But if he is able thus to contemplate the end of the world, it is because he began by contemplating its earliest beginnings. He looked, not like the neoclassicists, toward a golden age of civilization, but toward Chaos, Genesis, and Paradise. Blake looks for the original light in esotericism and eschatology: He heralds an end of the world that at the same time is a return to origins, a reincorporation into the first Eden. The revolution he proclaims is the completion of the great cycle. But although this belief concerns the whole human race, Blake expresses it in extremely individual language, whether poetical or pictorial. He speaks with a single lone voice of the fate of all; to the symbols of tradition he adds a symbolic language that is all his own; he is enigmatic while prophesying for the whole of mankind. Blake, an artist obsessed by the upsurge of light, becomes obscure not deliberately but in order to get as far away as possible from the error in which established societies and religions are imprisoned. Irreducible individualism, absolute singularity, what some might call madness casts a veil over what was intended to reveal the first and last truth.

THUS NEOCLASSICAL ART translated and transformed a passion for beginning into a nostalgia for beginning again. For these artists the light of the beginning could shine in the present only if it was a reflection of an absolute origin located in the past. A work of art was created far away from its real sources, in full awareness of the distance involved. But while works of this kind might have light, they lacked warmth: Art grew cold.

In some cases, no doubt, the memory of antique or Renaissance models might become a creative force, able to use a pure curve to express the moving equilibrium between presence and absence. But the multiform notion of the ideal as at once a purification of nature, a law of thought, and a canon of antiquity stopped the artist trusting to what he saw. Beauty yielded itself up only at second glance, after an excursion back in time to the realm of pure models or archetypes.

Clearly this was an attempt to reconcile the notion of beginning with the idea of the eternal. The neoclassical artists aimed at a revival different from the ephemeral fashions that made rococo intriguing. The "return to antiquity" was meant to be not a passing craze but a profound and serious conversion; not a novelty but an intermitting of the ceaseless quest for the curious, the new, and the unexpected on which the eighteenth century had frittered away its strength. Petty surprise was renounced in favor of the grandeur and harmony that transport without actually astonishing. It was a strange aspiration, and one which everything conspired to disappoint; for this desire for eternity in form appeared just when history was about to accelerate as never before.

Impulse was to be repressed and instinct mistrusted if it did not conform spontaneously to the norms of beauty. In fact, thought reigned supreme. For it knew it was trying, without "naiveté," to reconstruct a beauty which its creators in antiquity had "naively" invented. Beginning could be expressed only in allegory, in another language. And the distance was evident to those who wished most ardently to cross it. It was this inner dissonance that sometimes lent grace to their works and sometimes shocks our taste. Skill, artifice, and sensuality crept into "pure" line. Physical charm and real presence, superimposed on the ideal, ran the risk of seeming merely disturbing, like some obscene revenge of matter over spirit. Hence the striving after abstraction which banished color and shade from this kind of art; hence the triumph of drawing and line, though the ambiguity between "pure" line and sensual charm still survived. Empire and Georgian decorative artists made use of it, for a public whose love of pleasure was beginning to mask itself in hypocrisy. The art of the period frequently represented Psyche as the soul; but what it really depicted was adolescent nakedness offered up to a desire that was not of the soul.

GOYA

57)   FRANCISCO DE GOYA (1746–1828).
Charles IV of Bourbon, Equestrian. 1789.
(Madrid, Museo del Prado. Photo Anderson–Giraudon)

I N 1789 there was one painter who was hostile to idealizing abstraction and who remained so passionately attached to color and shade that he seems the absolute antithesis of all the neo-classicists dreamed of.[1] In his prodigious career Goya, rejecting the detour via antiquity, meditating on the mystery of matter both in the world and in painting, covered the whole distance between rococo and modern painting. To begin with he was influenced by Giaquinto, Luca Giordano, and Giambattista Tiepolo. After affecting for a long while to accept it, he threw off the tutelage of Mengs and of his own brother-in-law Francisco Bayeu. His most important works, produced after he was forty, are a lone and inspired anticipation of Manet, of expressionism, and of the audacities of the twentieth century. While in 1789 David, Canova, and Fuseli were already essentially what they would be until the end of their careers, Goya was to undergo an evolution that carried him a long way from the style of his early days. It is not only his deafness, after the illness that afflicted him in 1793, that reminds us of Beethoven, but also the extraordinary stylistic transformation he went through in the course of a few decades. Both artists, imprisoned in their solitude, created in their own works an independent world, using means that imagination, will, and a kind of inventive fury ceaselessly enriched and modified beyond all previous languages. Goya's modernity resides in this bold renewal forever leading him to an unknown universe and consigning him to an appalled confrontation with possible and impossible; it resides in the resolution with which he faced up to the pain of the historical moment using all the resources of his art and of his singular sensibility. He is one of the first artists to be driven by an imperative of perpetual progress vis-à-vis himself, to be always anxiously striving to break his own bounds. More than any previous painter he stood clear of the "taste" of his time. He renounced his first manner in order to be only himself, Goya, in total liberty of expression and in the loneliness of bearing inflexible witness. His life included both struggle and standing aside, both the profound originality of his pictorial language and the determination not to evade the sufferings of his country and of the age he lived in. Deeply intermingled, to the point of anguish, in his work, are concern with political liberty, a violent liberty of thematic imagination, and a liberty of "touch" that manifested itself in the very act of execution with brush, pencil, or pen. Goya's extreme independence of expression is the work of a man who experienced the greatest dependence. For Goya 1789 was the year which saw the belated consecration of his official career. He was appointed *pintor di cámara* to Charles IV, who had recently succeeded to the throne of Spain: He was to paint official portraits of the king and queen (figs. 57, 58). Success was assured; anyone else would have been lost. But Goya had a surplus of energy and a superabundant anxiety which could make themselves felt even in commissioned works. The painting of *St. Francis of Borgia and the Dying Man* gave him an opportunity to depict a vague group of grimacing devils around the second figure—the first appearance in his work of "monsters" and people with hallucinations. His por-

58) FRANCISCO DE GOYA (1746–1828).
Queen Maria Louisa in a Mantilla. 1789.
(Madrid, Museo del Prado. Photo Lauros-Giraudon)

59) FRANCISCO DE GOYA (1746–1828). *Self-portrait*. 1787.
(Castres, Musée des Beaux-Arts. Photo Musées Nationaux)

traits, like those of David, could bring out something impenetrable and anxious in the subject, sometimes even a kind of frozen aggression or potentiality for hate (fig. 59). True, he had learned, from a distance, the lesson of the English and French portrait painters: He was careful to enhance the model and wrap him or her in an aura of charm; he belonged to a period which rediscovered childhood, each individual's own Beginning and fleeting Golden Age. The children of the Duke of Osuna are shown in a misty atmosphere, but their somewhat melancholy look and shy fragility add an element of bitterness to the luminosity of the image (fig. 60).

For anyone able to decipher them, Goya's cartoons for the royal tapestry works, which occupied him from 1776 to 1792, are already "caprices." He produced genre scenes, scenes of popular life in Spain, according to the wishes of the prince and of the directors of the factory. The sixty or so cartoons, together with the preparatory sketches, show an evolution in technique and general tone, a growing luminosity, and an ever more assured ease and skill in composition. But let us concentrate rather on the constants. From the outset Goya shows people sunk in melancholy, scenes of violence, accidents, murders. Admittedly many scenes (those of the grape harvest, the flower girls, and children's games) strike us first of all by a graceful and almost gratuitous lightness, combining down-to-earth verismo with a somewhat facile charm (fig. 61). As in Fragonard—and Goya too painted swings—the scene seems to fix a moment when life fleetingly attains a plenitude of pleasure; in Goya's pictures, though, there is something less hasty and precipitate. But, as with Fragonard, we are sometimes haunted by the black reverse of what is shown in the bright opulence of the life of the senses. In the *Pradera of San Isidro* (1787)

60) FRANCISCO DE GOYA (1746–1828).
The Duke of Osuna and His Family.
(Madrid, Museo del Prado. Photo Anderson-Giraudon)

61) FRANCISCO DE GOYA (1746–1828). *The Grape Harvest.*
(Madrid, Museo del Prado. Photo Anderson-Giraudon)

Goya, while remaining himself, shares something with Fragonard, Hubert Robert, and Guardi: He depicts the melting away of a crowd, a multicolored murmur, by the way he manipulates a large space whose peacefulness contrasts with the excitement of the people (fig. 62). The parallel between the gentle sparkling of the river Manzanares and the soft glint of parasols and clothes is delightful. But what prevails in this human assembly is not happiness or single-minded fervor: The men and women there are exposing themselves to chance encounters; and everything suggests that the chance whose positive face we see has also a darker side. The artist who produced antithetical paintings of young and old women (now in the museum in Lille) already had a profound sense of the erosion of people and things. An essential instability, a potential disorder, foreshadow later festivities by Goya which will be returns to chaos. He brings to life a whole universe in the *Pradera*; and we know that in a whole universe evil and suffering must have a place. The tapestry cartoons are measured forerunners of this. In the pretty rhythms of *Blindman's Buff* we see a ludic transposition of a kind of torture, and the kneeling woman leaning back to avoid being touched seems to be fleeing from her own identity (fig. 63). There is another simulacrum of torture in *The Dummy*, where, while the laughing girls— young witches—form a garland with their arms, the slanting figure above them presents an aspect of despair (fig. 64). The twistedness, clumsiness, and painful inertia of this figure reveal the strange life that is in matter—its comic side, and its power to affright. The light-hearted scene contains a secret terror, in the life lent to a being entirely given over to its fate as an object. Here, in its deepest sense, we see the shadow, the darkness that neoclassical art tried to master or to banish, for to flee the dark obscurity of matter by means of pure form was the most constant ambition of that art. Goya may in fact have felt just as much dread as anyone before material darkness, but he chose to confront rather than repress it. But in 1789 there was as yet no sign of the scope of this confrontation: Goya was still only a painter in love with color who, like David, had learned to discipline the ardor of his first impulses. It took the combined effect of his illness in 1792–93, which left him deaf, and the great political upheaval of the day to make Goya's paintings and engravings openly reveal a disturbing element that had hitherto been hidden in the secret aura of his work. What in the cartoons had been no more than an intangible atmosphere now became a whole race of monsters, as if the principle of darkness had been condensed into spontaneous animation.

The unconscious seems to take over. At first sight the beholder may think that some deep disarray has gripped the painter's mind in a harsh and grotesque dream. But it would be anachronistic to apply to Goya an interpretation inherited from the romantic tradition and its surrealist surrogate. Goya's strangest works are not dictated merely by dream. They need to be understood in terms of a dual postulate arising out of the spirit of "enlightenment": the battle between darkness—that is, superstition, tyranny, and imposture—and the return to the source. As we shall see, it was a dual postulate that led to a hybrid creation.

[191]

62) FRANCISCO DE GOYA (1746–1828).
The Pradera of San Isidro. 1787.
(Madrid, Museo del Prado. Photo Giraudon)

63) FRANCISCO DE GOYA (1746–1828). *Blindman's Buff.*
(Madrid, Museo del Prado. Photo Anderson-Giraudon)

It was Goya the liberal, the friend of enlightened thinkers, who embarked on the denunciation of the evil, stupidity, and obstinacy of the henchmen of the Ancien Régime still lingering on in Spain. A man of reason, he would unmask the grotesque shapes born out of the sleep of reason. He would satirize night's phantoms. And while Fuseli deliberately refrained from anything misshapen or ignoble, Goya did not hesitate to carry sarcasm to the most violent extreme. To ridicule the creatures of night, he subjected them to a furious attack which itself had something nocturnal about it. The solar myth of the Revolution delighted in the insubstantiality of darkness: Reason had only to appear, supported by will, and darkness disappeared. As we have seen, the myth was an illusion. France experienced the intensest moments of its Revolution in a symbolism by which the light of principle merged into the opacity of the physical world and was lost. Goya, at a greater distance from the source of revolutionary light, was in a better position to describe the grimacing face of what absolutely rejected light. He angrily denounced this refractory element in the hope of arousing our destructive laughter. But in this case the satire actually confers being on what it aims to destroy and lends it a formidable solidity. Instead of executing justice, our laughter dies away and leaves us overwhelmed by strangeness and confronted by insuperable menace. The time was to come when the allusive shadows of *Blindman's Buff* became the horrible blindness of the singers in the *Quinta del Sordo* (1820). Goya's irony is unable to efface what it has created. Darkness has taken on a rough and massive self-evi-

64) FRANCISCO DE GOYA (1746–1828). *The Dummy.*
(Madrid, Museo del Prado. Photo Anderson-Giraudon)

dence that can no longer be sent back into the void. Reason is confronted with something radically different from reason: It knows the secret bonds that link it to these monsters, for they are born of its own demands, or rather of the rejection of its own demands. They represent the anarchic power of negation, which would not have appeared if the imperative of everyday order had not been proclaimed. This is an encounter fraught with consequences, for reason, seeing in its enemy the inversion of its own reality, the reverse without which reason would not be light, yields to the fascination of a difference it cannot escape. Goya does not believe in not believe in devils, but when he depicts the diabolical frenzy of those who still practice witchcraft, he flushes out a dim and obstinate stupidity that soon takes the form of devilish bestiality. Exorcism is once more necessary, though it is now entrusted to art. It consists in naming and tracing, by means of emblems or direct description, the innumerable shapes of evil, violence, and fatal madness.

Goya, as we have said, rejected the detour via antiquity that almost all his contemporaries regarded as a necessary condition in the quest for beauty. His work, like theirs, reveals a certain nostalgia for origins; but he was the only one, or almost the only one, who experienced the relationship with origins as a recourse to a spontaneous force; not as a quest, via the memory of learning, for a temporally privileged place (Arcadia) or an immutable form. For Goya, as for Diderot, and later for the romantics, origins were not an ideal principle but a vital energy. He examined this energy in the eyes of bulls, in the hair of the majas, in the mob, and in the colors of the world. To use a symbolic image, he left to others, to the "antiquaries" of Rome, the Greek god disguised as a beast, the mythological white bull, the ravisher of Europa. What he painted was the black beast that people slew in the village square. The origins he was concerned with were dark, with a deadly danger hovering over them. Life is close to death. And Goya's still lifes are terribly dead, all pulsation past, all "vital fluid" gone.

The denunciation of darkness brought forth a crowd of bestial beings. Recourse to origins meant a turning toward the deepest springs of life. And here we come to the point of hybridization, the strange confluence where in Goya's work the colors of life merged into the shadows of evil. Small wonder if the shapes condemned by reason are full of impetuous vitality, if images of origins are tainted by mocking horror. Thus there arose the grotesque and terrible image of a devouring origin—*Saturn*. Darkness and origins seem to intermingle in one great shipwreck. But in this Goya remains a faithful witness to the fate of the "enlightenment," the perverting of which he described as experienced by Spain in 1808. Revolutionary France, source of the light of principle, which Goya had hoped would radiate far and wide in peace, appears as a violent army, leaving murder and mindless rape in its wake. A baneful reversal had substituted darkness for light. Hope had been betrayed; history, which seemed to be advancing toward liberty, was losing its practical direction and becoming a crazy farce. Clearly we have here something different from what, in connection with neoclassical art, we called a return to darkness: What we are

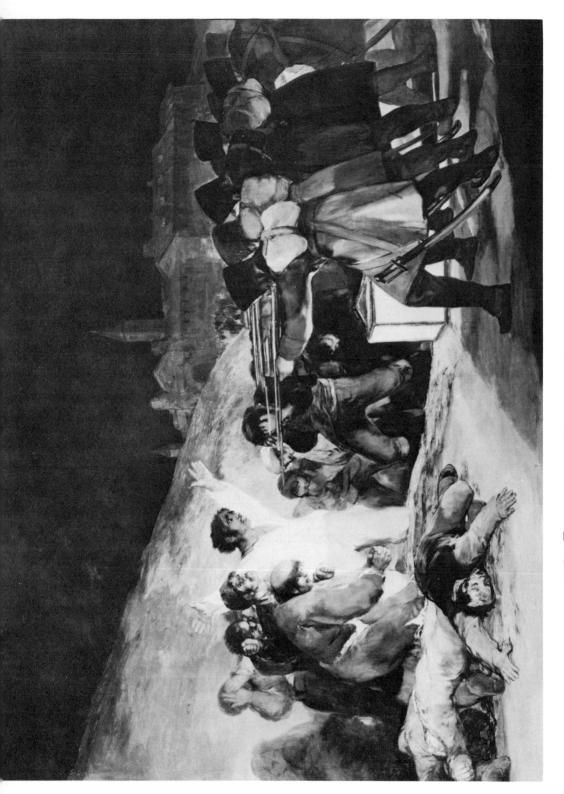

65) Francisco de Goya (1746–1828)
The Executions of 3 May 1808 in Madrid. 1814.
(Madrid, Museo del Prado. Photo Giraudon)

witnessing now is a genuine permutation replacing what once seemed a source of light by a source of darkness. We seem already to hear Goya uttering the cry of Gérard de Nerval in *Aurélia*: "The Universe is in Darkness!" I shall continue to examine Goya's later work because it shows the ultimate fate of what had been at stake in 1789. The culmination is to be seen in the picture showing the executions of May 3, 1808 (fig. 65). The rhythmic and disciplined group of the firing squad represents rationality gone mad; regularity and order, which should have marked the triumph of principle, serve only to regulate the wielding of violence. Goya's oblique treatment of the scene hides the faces of the French soldiers, who are seen only in profile, against the light of the sinister lantern at their feet. All we see of them is their equipment: guns, shakos, leather, greatcoats, and sabers. They are in the foreground, but everything about them corresponds to and harmonizes with the night sky dominating the background. Light, on the other hand, is linked to the group formed by the victims, especially to the man of the people who will be slain by the salvo about to be fired. Goya has managed to give his face, devoid of beauty, the simple expression that is at once beyond courage and beyond terror. With his arms outstretched as if he is being crucified, with his pierced hands, this rough-featured Spaniard suddenly takes on the aspect of the eternal Jew, of Man humiliated by man. For the beholder the light, though logically diffused from the lantern as its source, seems to emanate from the white shirt of the victim. We witness the tragedy of futile will and absolute impotence confronted by the mechanized will of the firing squad. But Goya makes us feel that this futile will, though powerless to ward off death, cannot be hurt or destroyed by it. He makes that will eternal. Not, as David immortalized Marat, a great man of the Revolution, by means of a solemn dedicatory inscription. What Goya is dealing with is someone obscure, of whose name and identity we are told nothing. In this way our attention is concentrated on the most basic of values, on the liberty inseparable from even the most commonplace existence. There is no clearer example of that aspect of the sublime which Kant defined in 1790 in his *Critique of Judgment*: Man discovers in himself a spiritual dimension by which he can outstrip the cosmic forces or historical aggressions that crush him.[2] Storm and tempest, like bullet and blade, herald the destruction of our physical existence but arouse in us the certainty that we may escape its limitations. Some late eighteenth-century landscape painters had tried to convey this kind of sublimity, but since most of them were bound by the conventions of "heroic landscape" and of studio composition, they had tended to ennoble and dematerialize the storms and tempests that were intended to make the beholder shudder. Only painters who could render all the wildness of the material world, all its mingled wealth of color, light, and shade, only painters like Goya, and sometimes David, have been able to depict the invisible presence of "moral liberty." For the highest freedom, both in the invention of form and in inner feeling, is given only to artists who have accepted the inevitabilities of matter and event and have been able boldly to take up their challenge.[3]

LIGHT

AND POWER

IN

The Magic Flute

_____

══════════

T HERE IS no lack of commentaries on *The Magic Flute*.[1] Goethe said it lent itself to a variety of different readings, giving simple pleasure to the majority and yielding up secret treasures to the initiate. Schikaneder's libretto is lively enough to fascinate an unsophisticated audience while at the same time conveying a complex allegory which, though its enigma is never wholly resolved, can be largely deciphered in terms of Masonic rites and dogmas. Over and above both the literal and the allegorical meanings, Mozart's music lends the opera an additional dimension of mystery and significance, designed at once to elude interpretation and inexhaustibly to challenge it.

Certainly, the central myth is that of the couple: The initiatory journey is at once a progress toward knowledge and a progress toward the highest kind of love. The series of tests is simultaneously the price that has to be paid in order to attain knowledge and the obstacle that must be overcome so that love may shine in its fullest joy. It is a very ancient theme, and one which has known some strange revivals: *The Woman without a Shadow*, by Hofmannsthal and Richard Strauss, is a reinterpretation of the same myth and consciously follows both *The Magic Flute* and Goethe's sequel to it.

But in addition to the first meaning, closely linking happiness with knowledge, we should look for another interpretation, one which poses a new question and brings out a meaning that has to do with power. Prob-

The text of this chapter is a lecture delivered to the Recontres Internationales de Genève, October 4, 1977.

ably we are drawn to this aspect nowadays because of the political preoccupations of our time. But this interest of ours is not an irrelevant question, ineptly imposed from without and anachronistic. Schikaneder and Mozart's singspiel is contemporary with the French Revolution: It poses, in the figurative form, the problem of authority and the basis of authority. If we listen carefully we notice the word *power* constantly recurring, closely associated with words expressing love, happiness, and knowledge.

There is nothing arbitrary or strained about raising the question of power in this context. The libretto is always talking about power; the word *Macht* continually crops up in both positive and negative form. Scene 1: Tamino, pursued by a snake, falls in a swoon, *fällt in Ohnmacht*. He is helped by the three veiled ladies sent by the Queen of the Night, who kill the monster with their silver spears and cry, "*Stirb, Ungeheu'r, durch unsre Macht*" ("Die, monster, by our power"). So much for the beginning. But at the end of the opera, power admits defeat, and again we hear the word *Macht*:

> Zerschmettert, zernichtet ist unsere Macht,
> Wir alle gestürzet in ewig Nacht.

So what we have witnessed in the course of the opera is a shift of power. The power that seemed so protective at the beginning is supplanted by a stronger and better power that marks the advent of universal happiness.

THE MAJOR and only real conflict is between the Queen of the Night and Sarastro, high priest of Wisdom and of the solar principle. Upon this conflict all the rest depends: In the first place the happiness of Tamino and Pamina, and secondly the fate of Papageno, anxious to find a mate. So we watch the proceedings of three couples, each at a different level of reality, proceedings affected by the assistance or resistance of minor characters, supernatural or priestly, acting under either the queen or Sarastro. These include the three ladies; the three boys; slaves, priests, and warders; armed men; and, more colorfully, the rebel slave who is Pamina's jailer and tormentor—the Moor Monostatos ("he who stands alone"), an image of perfidy and of the dark desires nurtured in anyone exercising delegated power.

Now I shall make use of an artifice. I examine the question of power in relation to each of the three couples in turn. In ascending order, from low to high; from pure instinct, which is close to the animal kingdom, to supreme wisdom.

Let us begin, then, with Papageno, the part that Schikaneder, the librettist, wrote for himself. He stands for vital energy, spontaneous but primitive—the part of man that will never be admitted to initiation. But it is through Papageno that the solemn allegory is punctuated and relieved by clowning, by moving moments interspersed with comic scenes. Goethe liked this swift alternation of atmosphere and deliberately strove for the same effect in the sketch he intended as a sequel to *The Magic Flute*. Between simple fun and the mysteries of the universe the distance is great and the oscillation startling. But the spectator, passing thus from dread to laughter, from meditation to easy jest, runs the whole gamut of human emotion and sees himself entire.

Papageno, a birdcatcher, twittering like a bird even

when his lips are padlocked, bearing the name of a bird, a man of nature (*Naturmensch*), unable to hide his cowardice, greed, and love of girls, is a character whose meaning we can guess at once. From every point of view he is the man of spontaneous desire, of instinct, of thought that is brief and artless. He is quite willing to pass himself off as having bested the snake, to be credited with a power he does not possess. Even his claim to mere physical strength is an empty one.

So can we really speak of power in relation to him? Perhaps we need to define our terms more closely and keep the word *power* for effective authority which imposes order. Power produces, willingly or otherwise, justly or unjustly, subordination. We may then use the word *force*, or *strength*, for the individual's ability to manifest himself in accordance with his own energies; this force, this strength may be restricted to the individual himself and not seek to subordinate others. Admittedly, every being conscious of his strength is tempted to turn it into a source of power, by organizing a world that will be obedient to his will.

All that Papageno reigns over is the cageful of birds he carries on his back. So his power is absurd; and it is a power innocently cruel, the power of imprisoning animals. Yet there is in him an irrepressible force, that of primitive life with its simple pleasures, its fleeting woes, its perfect health. (Mozart, on his deathbed, asked for Papageno's songs, which are the very warmth of life, to be sung to him.) This absence of extensive power, this spontaneous force, can be summed up in the simple concept of immediacy. This type of immediacy had already been often depicted in the eighteenth century in the form of the noble savage or of Harlequin (and such counterparts of the latter as Kasperl). Papageno, the parrot-man, is simultaneously noble savage and Kasperl; in addition, if we follow Chailley in applying the code of alchemy to the characters in *The Magic Flute*, he has a close affinity to one of the four elements, Air. This class of characters is in close contact with the animal world, both because of their instinct and because they live among the brute beasts. It is important here to stress the quality of immediacy, for in the opera it contrasts with the mediate character of the initiatory experience imposed on Tamino and Pamina.

All Papageno knows of the world is a limited area: He is familiar with no other country but his own little valley. He is content with a straw hut and lives from hand to mouth. Birdcatching, a primitive mode of subsistence, is the only work he knows; let others build churches. The rudimentary economic activity of bartering, with the queen's ladies, provides him with his daily bread. Above all, Papageno's desires know only short-term satisfaction; he forms no long-term plans. As a result, when any pleasure offers he sees no need to put off enjoying it, no need to suppress the thought of it or go beyond it. Rousseau had described in exactly the same terms the happiness and the stupidity of the man of nature. But although Papageno is ineducable, he does possess an elementary erotic force that promises happiness at a certain low level. The horde of little Papagenos and Papagenas which the couple promise themselves and which Mozart's music expresses with such irony bears witness to vital fertility and animal health. Papageno, who himself cannot attain the life of the spirit, is the energy out of which the life of the spirit can and will arise. Just as Leporello has been seen as Don Giovanni's double, or shadow, so, in terms of our modern psychological dictionaries, we may see Papageno as the double, or id, of Tamino: It is only a partial and rudimentary correspondence, but one on which all the rest may be built, given effort, toil, and the braving of obstacles.

One last comment on Papageno, to show how typical he is of the traditional theatrical clown. The clown, though not directly involved in the plot, intervenes in it either as an aid or as a hindrance. Sometimes his untimely interference is providential; then he is an unwitting savior or rescuer. Such is Papageno. Sent as herald and messenger by Tamino, he twice arrives just at the right moment to save Pamina from the tender mercies of the dark and violent Monostatos. And it is Papageno who reveals Tamino's love to Pamina before Tamino himself appears. Papageno's words play the same role vis-à-vis the heroine as Pamina's portrait vis-à-vis the hero: He announces a love object while at the same time underlining its absence. Although Papageno has no direct power, his innocence and gaiety—helped along by pipe and glockenspiel—are turned into indirect power: All unaware, he turns the wheel of fate.

Now let us go higher up the ladder, to the rung that belongs to Tamino and Pamina. What happens to them shows us how power may be attained.

Tamino is the son of a prince, and at the beginning of the opera he is being pursued by a monster. He is about to die and calls for help.

He falls in a swoon.[2] And from this temporary void he comes back to life not knowing where he is or who it was that saved him. He is in a situation of weakness and dependence, in the depths of error, illusion, and credulity. Power lies at the end of a path that begins in darkness.

It is as a man, not as the son of a king, that Tamino undergoes the ordeals of initiation. The libretto stresses the theme of equality. On the other hand, Sarastro tells Tamino that if he comes through the ordeal successfully he will reign in future as a wise prince: "*als ein weiser Prinz zu regieren.*" The apprenticeship of mankind as a whole is the same as these particular preparations for the exercise of the best possible power, power fully legitimate. Certain productions, like those of Bergman, do not hesitate to stress this justified accession to power in the last scene. The withdrawal of Sarastro renders the contrast as great as possible between Tamino's initial powerlessness and his final omnipotence. Moreover, the accession to power coincides with the fulfillment of the couple's love in full spiritual maturity, victorious over darkness, silence, and misunderstanding. Thus the loftiest synthesis of love takes place at the same time as the conquest of knowledge and power. All desirable happinesses merge into a single shining mass, the sum of all the fantasies of youth.

It is well-known that the ordeals Tamino undergoes correspond closely to Masonic ritual. I shall not go into the various stages of the journey through the labyrinth. For my present purposes, the symbolic detail of those stages is less important than the principle behind the test—a journey in which the hero is called upon to develop and enter into possession of a spiritual strength of which he was hitherto unaware.

The Masonic religion, which aims at ushering a new era into the world, also sees itself as inspired by the most ancient truths. Its ordeal ritual is borrowed from the mystery cults of antiquity, though also influenced by certain practices of medieval chivalry. The symbolism of a voyage toward truth or holiness could be exploited almost in its entirety by the thought of the Enlightenment to depict the gradual discovery of the voice of conscience, the patient progress by which non-reason—animal, helpless, aimless—becomes Reason, stable and in control of its own power. The *roman d'éducation* was a narrative version of what *The Magic Flute* offers in the form of solemn and yet fairy-tale lyricism. *Sethos*, by the Abbé Terrasson, to which the libretto of the opera owes a good deal, was a novel of this kind. Terrasson, a strong supporter of the moderns, gave his message an imaginary setting in Ancient Egypt, formulating his rationalist beliefs amid the temples of Isis and Osiris; a strange compromise between ancient myth and new philosophy. Rousseau's *Emile* and Goethe's *Wilhelm Meister* both show the journey through the contemporary world of someone learning to enter into possession of his own freedom. At the time, many people believed that the whole of mankind could benefit from this kind of education, which would transform a merely confused awareness into a reason in control of its own will and identity. The myth of human progress, which came to the fore just at that time, applies to the future of the whole human race the promise of freedom which the educational novel restricts to

the fate of a single individual. The series of tests is
paralleled by the slow march of history toward fulfillment and the reconciliation of all those hitherto separated by ignorance. If we read over the libretto of *The
Magic Flute*, we find the promise made to Tamino and
Pamina repeated twice in the same terms. The happiness awaiting them is the happiness of the whole world,
a new golden age. At the end of the first act the priests
sing:

> When virtue and justice
> Shed glory over this noble path,
> The earth is a kingdom of heaven
> And mortals are like gods.
>
> (Wenn Tugend und Gerechtigkeit
> Den Grossen Pfad mit Ruhm bestreut,
> Dann ist die Erd' ein Himmelreich
> Und Sterbliche den Göttern gleich.)[3]

And the three boys repeat the last two lines at a
turning point in the story (2:26), heralding the imminent victory of the sun, the destruction of superstition,
and the return of "sweet serenity" (*holde Ruhe*). "*Soon
the earth will be a heavenly kingdom.*" I propose to
take this phrase as an eschatological promise, in perfect
accord with the myth of dawn and solar victory that
was widespread in the early years of the Revolution. (It
has been said that the Freemasonry of the eighteenth
century, which aimed at being purely moral and not
political, nevertheless gave rise to a radical critique of
the state as an institution and that its influence was all
the more political for claiming to be nonpolitical: According to the historian Reinhart Koselleck, this

amounted to drawing a blank check on the future without having any political funds in the bank.)[4]

When the singspiel ends in triumph we see how far we have come since the bewilderment of the beginning. The journey reveals the function performed by love in the shaping of personal identity. For what made Tamino set out on his quest was first of all the awakening of desire at the sight of the portrait of Pamina sent him by the Queen of the Night. Tamino is ready to face anything in order to be with the person whose image bewitched him. His only purpose is to free her from Sarastro, whom the queen has denounced as a tyrant. The primal force which leads Tamino into adventure is an instinct, or drive. Schikaneder several times repeats the word *Trieb*, later used by Freud. But we are not straining the interpretation of *The Magic Flute* if we make use of another Freudian idea and say that Tamino's initiation is nothing other than the sublimation of this original desire. In the course of his journey the hero changes his goal, aims higher, though without renouncing the first object of his desire, which becomes what the psychoanalysts call a "secondary gain": "May the knowledge of wisdom be my victory, and sweet Pamina my reward" (2:3). Possession of the loved one thus ceases to be the immediate aspiration. Tamino agrees to defer it. He agrees to let the risk of death and the constraint of silence come between him and the one he loves. In return for absence and pain he wins a redoubled presence; thus renunciation (unknown to Papageno) opens up for him the dimension of the future. One must impose the worst frustration on oneself to give proof of an inner strength and thus enter into possession of power extending far beyond the small circle of immediate satisfaction. The love of Tamino and Pamina now has both a past and a future: It has overcome despair and death, and nothing can endanger it any more.

But the temporary break that Tamino consciously submits to in the hope of future compensation is seen by Pamina as an incomprehensible disaster. The pathos of the heroine is linked to the ruthlessness with which she is persecuted by fate, so that, until the successful denouement, she is a victim upon whom all possible misfortune falls without her understanding anything about it. She has lost a beloved father, a mysterious character whom she cherishes in her memory. She has been reft from her mother, the *sternflammende Königin*, whom she persists in thinking of as a loving parent. She is the prisoner of the unknown but powerful Sarastro, who has not revealed his ultimately kind intentions. She has to bear the brutish advances of Monostatos. Tamino, who she thinks loves her, is silent, then bids her a last farewell. She tries to kill herself, but the three boys prevent her at the last moment. Her frustration is great, unceasing, repeated. Pamina is surrounded by an aura reminiscent of "shockers" and other Sade-like imaginings. White daughter of a dark mother, she is sister to Fuseli's tormented sleepers, and to all the frail creatures cruelly sequestered in the Gothic dungeons and Inquisition cells of the late eighteenth-century novel. The pathos of captivity gave rise to a special type of musical work—the opera of "rescue" (*Rettungsoper*), of which Berton's *Rigueurs du Cloître* was an early example and

Fidelio one of the last. Constance, in *The Abduction from the Seraglio*, had already been a prisoner, and her fate too had invited reflection on the abuse of power.

But the series of sorrows inflicted on Pamina is also a test, a journey of initiation—a double one, even, for as well as passing from the nocturnal, feminine realm of her mother into the solar, masculine realm of Sarastro, she also traverses darkness and death, thus becoming worthy of crossing, with Tamino, the sacred threshold. The suffering endured is the price paid for the acquisition of power. In the last ordeal Pamina takes Tamino's hand and guides him. Love, when purified by endurance, is no longer the instinctive impulse that needs to be overcome, but instead a directing force, a strength that can act as a guide through flood and fire. Pamina sings:

> I lead you,
> Love guides me.
> (Ich selbsten führe dich
> Die Liebe leitet mich.)

But love is not the only power that can guide. At this moment the magic flute protects the couple and shows them the way. The verb *leiten*, whose first subject was love, *die Liebe*, is repeated, this time with the flute as subject. Pamina sings:

> Tamino, take your flute and play,
> That it may lead us along this dark path.
> (Nun komm und spiel die Flöte an,
> Sie leite uns auf grauser Bahn.)

Then both sing:

> Through the power of music we complete our journey,
> Cheerfully through the dark Night of Death!
> (Wir wandeln durch des Tones Macht
> Froh durch des Todes düst're Nacht!)
>
> [2:28]

It is at this moment, incidentally, that we learn from Pamina's lips the origin of the flute given to Tamino by the Queen of the Night. "My father carved it, in an enchanted hour, from the deepest heart of an ancient oak" (2:28). In terms of modern psychology, one is tempted to see the magic flute as an emblem of the archaic father giving his consent and protection to the new couple: The strength they have acquired goes back to a benevolent ancestral past. But a psychoanalytical interpretation of the symbol would omit what is most important if it made us forget the interpretation that was quite obvious to Mozart's contemporaries: The flute signifies harmony—not only the harmony of the couple, but also, much more fundamentally, the harmony of the world. Harmony is the basic organizing principle, and so power par excellence. It is through harmony that chaos may become order. Jean-Philippe Rameau, in his theoretical writings, was always saying that the "law of harmonic generation" produced by the vibration of an instrument was the fundamental secret of the universe, the source of all geometrical, optical, and moral proportion. The Freemasons applied the idea generally. Mesmer, the hypnotist, extended it to medicine. According to him animal magnetism is a universal fluid that acts rhythmically in the cosmos and in our bodies. His treatment claimed to restore a propitious harmony between the body and the universe. Some of the more enthusiastic of his followers thought individual health was inconceivable except in terms of the harmony of society as a whole. (The reader will hardly need reminding that Mozart had met Mesmer and that *Bastien und Bastienne* was commissioned by him. Also, a "mesmeric compass" is a comical property in *Così fan tutte*, used by Despina to cure the Albanians of their feigned poisoning. More seriously, the magical effect on animals of Tamino's flute at the end of Act 1, scene 15, can be explained as a reminiscence of Orpheus.) The flute and the power of music are kept for the last test, the most difficult of all. So, because harmony is the law of the universe, the moral rule, the instrument Tamino plays is not a mere instrument to use as he wills. It is power itself—a gentle power, without violence—of which Tamino is only the agent and by which he lets himself be guided. What the final test stands for is not merely the triumph of love: It is also the triumph of music and the musician.

I SHOULD BE HARD PUT to give my argument any philosophical consistency. I have just said that the higher power which conquers and triumphs was the power of harmony, symbolized by the flute. And this is an impersonal power—served by a person but quite distinct from that person. But I said before that spiritual strength, the strength arising out of the rejection of immediate desire, the strength that accepts and interiorizes the risk of death, is changed into power, that is, into the ability to impose order on other beings after having imposed it on oneself. In this case, power is linked to a person; its source lies in the "virtuous" mind of an individual who has been able to deny himself and emerge successful from the most searching trials. Have I not put forward two contradictory theories as to the source or basis of power? Yet we have to admit that the dream (or Utopia) of Enlightenment philosophy was to be able to reconcile these two apparently conflicting propositions. And this is nowhere more evident than in the character of Sarastro.

Where do power and authority reside? There are two possible answers. One is a soothing answer and says that power belongs to the gods—Isis and Osiris—and the order of the stars. The source of authority is among the great impersonal eternal entities: light, wisdom, virtue, love, harmony, and so on. In order to act among men, transcendent law needs an interpreter, and none but perfect beings can perform this function: Sarastro is only an agent. But however hard this theocracy tries to be rational (as distinct from the law that derives from "revelation"), can it throw off the suspicion that Enlightenment philosophy always harbored vis-à-vis the power of kings and priests? And now for a less soothing answer—indeed, a heretical one as compared with the intentions of the libretto of *The Magic Flute*: Anyone who tries to pass himself off as the interpreter of a universal and impersonal power is only trying to make respectable and sacrosanct decisions based on his own wishes and dictated by self-interest alone. In short: Enlightenment philosophy rebelled against the arbitrary exercise of power as wielded by absolute monarchs; it wanted to transfer that power to a universal and impersonal principle (such as natural law, reason, the general will, the people, and so on). Universal obedience to one impersonal law is the very definition of equality. But then there arose the problem of the person or persons who set up to be legitimate interpreters of the universal principle. The traditional Enlightenment criticism of the imposture of clerics could be applied even more severely against Robespierre when he claimed to be high priest of the Supreme Being.

But, to return to the power of Sarastro: Sarastro (whose name echoes that of Zoroaster or Zarathustra) is not a king but a high priest. The only things above him are the gods and their laws, of which he is the interpreter. In the famous aria "Under these sacred vaults" (*In diesen heil'gen Hallen*), Sarastro's main point is that vengeance is unknown there (*Kennt man die Rache nicht*) (2:12). Vengeance is nothing other than the expression of personal wish. The initiate has abdicated this wish or passion to be merely the officiant of a compassionate and disinterested law. (The enemies—the Queen of the Night, Monostatos—know only selfish passion: jealousy, anger, murder, revenge.)

Sarastro, with his magic talisman—the "sevenfold ring of the sun," which extends the seven notes of the scale to planetary space—has some of the attributes of divinity: He can see everything throughout all space and time. Like the divinity, he has no history of his own. (At the other extreme, Papageno has to all intents and purposes no history, being close to the animal world, with only short-term aspirations dictated by physical appetite.) Nothing can happen to Sarastro. No danger can threaten him. He has won in advance. The

Queen of the Night is subject to his power from the start (1:18). He knew in advance that Tamino and Pamina were destined for each other; he is aware of the wicked designs of Monostatos; he knows the secrets of other people's hearts; in the marvelous trio where he decrees that the lovers shall be parted, he knows already that they will be reunited. *Wir sehn us wieder* (2:21).

One cannot help thinking here of the scene in Rousseau's *Emile*, where the tutor separates Emile and Sophie and watches them say goodbye, knowing full well, though he alone is aware of it, that this is only a prelude to the joy of reunion.

Like Rousseau's tutor, Sarastro secretly controls all the action: He has a plan of his own, revealed to the others only in the moment of its fulfillment. In it he manipulates the enemy forces to his own advantage. The negative powers unwittingly serve his purposes. So he is powerful enough himself never to need to resort to violence. The words most often in his mouth, like a direct manifestation of his power, are "lead" and "guide," *führen* and *leiten*. His orders are obeyed to the letter by a host of priests, warders, and messengers, who while praying to the gods never omit to pay homage to Sarastro, the personal tributes they pay him sometimes even suggesting what is now called a "personality cult":

> It is him we joyfully obey.
> He is our idol, to whom all devote themselves.
> (Er ist es, dem wir uns mit Freude ergeben.
> Er ist unser Abgott, dem alle sich weihn.)
>
> [1:18]

Sarastro, the ominiscient, almost divine teacher whose hidden hand controls all the action, belongs to a group of characters onto whom, from Fénelon's *Télémaque* on, Enlightenment philosophy projected its dream of an effective wisdom that could lead mankind to knowledge and happiness. Nowadays people ask disrespectfully whether such benevolent characters are not really "authoritarian personalities." For all their benevolence, are they not, with their promises to the young of power in exchange for repression or frustration, mere manipulators? (I deliberately use the vocabulary now in fashion, arising out of a mythology of desire and dream and regarding all rational constraint as oppressive.)

But the figure of Sarastro reaches its greatest heights at the symbolic level. His conflict with the Queen of the Night is the conflict between light and darkness; also, secondarily, the conflict between male and female. The Queen of the Night is the most difficult character to interpret. What does she stand for? The Catholic Church and, more generally, the political authorities hostile to Freemasonry? The women's lodges, which rivaled the men's?[5] The spirit of evil? I am not going to suggest a new interpretation. I accept without further ado the literal image of a cosmic power—the starry night, with its infinite sparkling riches. I also agree to see her as the bad mother (the mother with the "bad breast"), who to regain her power is prepared to sacrifice her daughter and deliver her over to the loathsome Monostatos. One of the symbolical attributes of night is the veil. Not only are all her serving ladies veiled, but the queen's method of trying to recover her power is a sort of veiling. She slanders Sarastro and the initiates; she says they are hypocritical imposters and monsters. The first test Tamino and Pamina pass through successfully consists in lifting this veil of untruth, which at first had prevented them from seeing the true faces, friendly and human, of the disciples of Wisdom. Even after the veil has been pierced, there are still a number of obstacles between the seekers and a truth that eludes direct approach. The figure of the queen, at first thought to be propitious but subsequently seen as hostile, determines the dramatic tension. First she helps, then she hinders, thus multiplying the illusions, errors, and obstacles which lengthen the initiatory journey and increase the value of the ultimate victory.

A victory is only glorious when the enemy forces are sufficiently strong. So it was important not to reveal the "original" inferiority of the queen too soon; and the best way to prevent her being seen as vanquished from the beginning was to make her a temporarily generous and beneficent power in the first part of the opera.

Woman, denigrated in the person of the queen, gets her own back in the queen's daughter Pamina, albeit through obedience to the law of initiation, which is masculine.[6] Woman is welcomed in the person of Pamina, relegated to the abyss in the person of the queen and her aides. For the young couple there is reconciliation, but the dark widow, the sublimely singing witch, seems to disappear forever. The queen, Monostatos, and the veiled ladies will have served only to underline the victory of Sarastro. The eye may follow, against the darkness, the rising of the sun, but when the sun appears the darkness melts away. In moral and political terms, we have to invent a negative principle strong enough to explain why the light of justice is not present from the beginning in every man's heart. The reason why the human world is not yet resplendent with light is that the Prince (here the princess) of Darkness prevents it. Every eschatology, every Utopia, has to invent the face of an enemy, so as to blame him for the delay in the advent of universal happiness. So every Utopia is Manichaean. But Manichaeanism derives from Zoroastrianism, so Sarastro's name is perfectly apt.

AT THE END OF *The Magic Flute*, space is full of the chords of a shining glory in E-flat, a key beloved of the Freemasons. It is the Parousia, the end of the world. Can one imagine a sequel to *The Magic Flute?* Goethe dreamed of composing a similar work to be performed by other musicians. How did he go about it?

If we look at the many works that around 1789 tried to convey an image of light triumphant in its struggle aginst darkness, we see that in the productions of the great artists darkness is never completely expelled; somehow it always returns to the charge. Mozart and Schikaneder knew this and made the dark Monostatos a servant of Sarastro (nowadays some would use Jung's term and call him Sarastro's *shade*). Similarly, on the political scene, the French Revolution first saw itself as a great dawn for the human race. Then it was gradually overtaken by suspicion, by obsession with the enemy within, by terror. (Saint-Just said: "Our aim is to establish an order of things which will in turn establish a universal bent toward good; which will bring faction swiftly to the scaffold.")[7]

Goethe made use of this law, the law of the return of darkness, in the fragment he composed as a sequel to Mozart's opera. What we see first is an apparent victory for Night. Monostatos, on the queen's orders, has introduced himself into Tamino's royal palace, seized Pamina's newborn child, and, unable to carry it off, shut it up in a golden coffin sealed with the seal of the Queen of the Night. The king and Pamina are in despair; they mourn separately, each alone. If the child is to stay alive inside the coffin, the coffin has to be carried night and day. Sarastro has to lay aside his power; fate dooms him to perform a year's pilgrimage among men—outside the overprotected walls of the temple. He is welcomed in the cottage of Papageno and Papagena, who have no children and lament the barrenness of their marriage. Sarastro produces some children from ostrich eggs, a somewhat disconcerting skill. The last scene Goethe wrote—though not the end of the piece—takes us into a shrine and shows us the opening of the coffin. The child is still alive. Goethe calls it Genius. But the genius takes flight and disappears into thin air. Many themes in the *Second Faust*—including the homunculus and the flight of Euphorion—are foreshadowed here. We do not know for certain how Goethe might have finished his piece. The surviving images are centrifugal: Sarastro leaves the temple; the child, delivered from its dark prison, flies upward and vanishes. *The Magic Flute* itself ended in a marvelously convergent movement, a radiant center, as if the world was at last about to attain its immutable truth. Goethe's fragment calls everything back into question. He takes the same mythical characters, the same conflict between light and darkness, but makes them into an enigmatical fragment expressing the dark, problematical, shifting aspect of the beginning of the modern world. The questions it poses remain unanswered. Can Genius perhaps be an inhabitant of the earth? Can a wise man retain power? When the "master of wisdom" agrees to a life of wandering and pilgrimage, we witness the complete reversal of the certainty proclaimed in the aria Mozart gives to Sarastro. After the master's departure the choir sings:

> Es soll die Wahrheit
> Nicht mehr auf Erden
> In voller Klarheit
> Verbreitet werden.
> Dein hoher Gang
> Ist nun vollbracht;
> Doch uns umgibt
> Die tiefe Nacht.[8]

(Truth will no more stretch over the earth in its fine splendor. Your lofty journey is now completed. Deep night surrounds us.)

In our age of exiled truth, we feel this sad choir speaks with our own voice. And that is why our eyes may fill with tears when Mozart sings of the imminence of dawn—this *bald*, this "soon," which did not come in our century: *Die düst're Nacht verscheucht der Glanz der Sonne. Bald fühlt der edle Jüngling neues Leben* (2:20). "The splendor of the sun drives away the dark night. Soon the noble youth will know the new life." We are still waiting for the new life.

Notes and Additions

Short Bibliography

Index of Names

66) HUBERT ROBERT (1733–1808).
The Germinal Hallway at St.-Lazare. 1794.
(Paris, Musée Carnavelet. Photo Bulloz)

Notes and Additions

1789

1. Barnave, a member of the Constituent Assembly, wrote a remarkable *Introduction to the French Revolution*, analyzing it in the light of the economic history of Europe since the Renaissance:

"In the governments of Europe the basis of aristocracy is land ownership, the basis of monarchy is public authority, and the basis of democracy personal wealth.

"Revolutions in these three political factors have corresponded to revolutions in government.

"When the energy of the feudal regime was at its height, the only property was in land; the equestrian and ecclesiastical aristocracy dominated everything, the people were reduced to slavery, and the princes no longer had any power.

"The renaissance in the arts brought with it the industrial and personal property which is the fruit of labor, just as land ownership was originally the result of conquest or occupation.

"The democratic principle, then almost stifled, has since never ceased to develop and grow stronger. As arts, industry, and commerce have enriched the working class, impoverished the great landowners, and brought the classes nearer to each other in wealth, so educational progress has brought them closer together in manners, and has reintroduced, after a long period of oblivion, the old ideas about equality. . . .

"Almost everywhere, natural causes were aided by the influence of royal power, which, having long been oppressed by the aristocracy, called the people to its rescue. For a long while the people acted as an auxiliary to the throne against their common enemies; but when it was strong enough to be no longer satisfied with a subordinate role, it exploded and took its place in government" (*Introduction à la Révolution française*, Foreword by F. Rude [Paris, 1960], chaps. 5 and 12).

2. While Barnave saw the Revolution as the ultimate explosion of a principle whose victory, for economic reasons, had been in preparation for centuries, the theosophist Louis-Claude de Saint-Martin tried to see it as a mysterious decree of Providence. He was an enemy of the church and its priests and looked forward to the triumph of true theocracy:

"When I consider the beginnings of the French Revolution and the moment when it actually began to explode, I find no apter comparison than with a reduced image of the Last Judgment, where the trumpets utter imposing sounds dictated to them by a superior voice; where all the powers of earth and heaven are overthrown, and the just and the unjust receive their reward in the twinkling of an eye. For, apart from the crises by which physical nature seemed to prophesy the Revolution, did not all the great ones and higher orders of the state take flight when the Revolution actually broke out, driven out by terror alone, without any other pursuer than an invisible hand? Did not the oppressed, as through some supernatural power, take back all the rights usurped from them by injustice?

"When we look at the Revolution as a whole and the swiftness of its development . . . we are tempted to compare it to a feat of magic or a theatrical 'spectacle'; and this has led someone to say that only the same hidden hand that directed the Revolution could write its history" (*Lettre à un ami ou considérations politiques, philosophiques et religieuses sur la Révolution française* [Paris, an III], pp. 12–13).

THE FREEZE

1. Robert's *Démolition de la Bastille*, with its great corner tower, the shadow falling on the fortress walls, and the smoke hanging over what is going on in the background, is an admirable piece of work. Symbol is more important in it than fidelity to fact.

The man himself was thought to be worldly and rather superficial. "Of all the artists I have known," says Mme Vigée-Lebrun in her *Souvenirs*, "Robert was the one most widely seen in society, of which by the way he was very fond. He was a connoisseur of all pleasures, not excluding those of the table, and was much sought after; I do not think he dined at home three times a year. Theaters, balls, banquets, concerts, picnics—he refused nothing; all the time he did not spend working he spent enjoying himself.

"He had natural wit and learning without pedantry, and the unquenchable cheerfulness of his personality made him the most agreeable person possible in society. He was always famous for his skill in every kind of physical activity, and even when quite advanced in years lost none of the predilections of his youth. When he was over sixty and become very fat, he was still so agile he could run faster than anyone in a race, he played tennis and football, and delighted us with schoolboy tricks that made us laugh till we cried. One day, for example, at Colombes, he drew a long chalk line on the drawing-room floor; then, dressed up as a tumbler, and holding a balancing pole, he started to walk, to run, solemnly along the line, imitating the positions and attitudes of a tight-rope walker so well that the illusion was perfect, and no one had ever seen anything so funny" (E. Vigée-Lebrun, *Souvenirs*, 2 vols. [Paris, Charpentier, n.d.], 2:329).

Hubert Robert was arrested "on suspicion" on October 29, 1793. He was imprisoned first at Sainte-Pélagie and then at

Saint-Lazare, and not released until after the 9 Thermidor. He did not stop painting while in prison. Mme Vigée-Lebrun claims he had been denounced by David, but this seems unlikely.

See a recent monograph by Bernard de Montgolfier, "Hubert Robert, peintre de Paris au musée Carnavalet," *Bulletin de musée Carnavalet*, nos. 1 and 2, 1964; also C. Gabillot (1895), and P. de Nolhac (1910).

For the hostility that the "Commune des arts," soon to become the "Société populaire et républicaine des arts," showed, for civic and moral reasons, towards genre painters and artists who did not devote their talents to the service of the revolutionary idea, see H. Lapauze, *Procès-verbaux de la Société populaire et révolutionnaire des arts* (Paris, 1903). For a fair appraisal of the part played by David, see Louis Hautecoeur, *Louis David* (Paris, 1954); also the book by D. L. Dowd.

2. Jacques-Henri Bernardin de Saint-Pierre, *Œuvres*, 2 vols., vol. 1 (Paris, 1840), p. 669.

3. The solitary outcast described by Bernardin de Saint-Pierre in *La Chaumière indienne* (The Indian Cottage) knows true happiness and possesses perfect wisdom. The idea of happiness in obscurity, of a retreat into wild and primitive nature, was still attractive in the years around 1789. We know that in the middle of the Revolution the young Senancour answered the call and went to dream in the Swiss Alps, vaguely hoping for more distant horizons, in the direction of the South Sea Islands. But the pursuit of a refuge in nature is not incompatible with a social Utopia. Senancour several times (between 1797 and 1798) asked the Directors to help him carry out his project of establishing on a Pacific island "a happy institution, a first example for the social universe." See *Sur les Générations actuelles: Absurdités humaines* (1793), preface by Marcel Raymond (Geneva, 1963), p. xx. See also Marcel Raymond's penetrating *Senancour* (Paris, 1965), and Béatrice Didier–Le Gall's two volumes *L'Imaginaire chez Senancour* (Paris, 1966).

4. To justify the language of symbols (which was to be the language of the Revolution), Bernardin de Saint-Pierre used the example of light, which is only visible to us by contact with the objects that intercept it:

"We should not see the light of the sun if it was not encountered by bodies, or at least by clouds. It escapes us outside of our own atmosphere, and dazzles us at its source. The same is true of truth; we should not be able to grasp it if it did not fix itself on tangible events, or at least on metaphors and comparisons which reflect it; it needs a body from which to rebound. Our understanding can get no grip on purely metaphysical truths, it is dazzled by those emanating from the Divinity, and cannot grasp those which do not rest on His works. . . .

"Just as the clouds, scattered in a thousand fantastic forms, sometimes break down the rays of the sun into hues more rich and varied than those which color the ordinary works of nature, so fables reflect truth more amply than real events. They transport it into all the orders of nature, associating it with animals, trees, and the elements, and making it give forth countless reflections. So sun-rays play without being extinguished under water, reflecting objects in earth and sky, and increasing their beauty with parallels.

"Thus ignorance is as necessary to truth as darkness is to light, since the first of these pairs form the harmonies of our intelligence just as the second form those of our sight" (Foreword, *La Chaumière indienne*, 1791). The function ascribed to darkness in the formation of colors recalls Goethe's theory on the subject.

5. Jean-Paul Rabaut Saint-Etienne, *Précis historique de la Révolution française, Assemblée constituante*, 6th ed. (Paris, 1813), p. 61.

6. Beaumarchais, *Le Mariage de Figare*, act 5, scene 3.

7. Madame de Staël, "Considérations sur la Révolution française," *Œuvres complètes*, 2 vols. (Paris, 1836), 2:299.

8. Rabaut Saint-Etienne, pp. 107–8.

9. In his *Considérations sur l'Esprit et les Mœurs* (1787), Sénac de Meilhan imagines that a time of satiety, disgust, and boredom is not far off. Knowledge and art have developed as far as they can, and man is doomed to apathy in a world where everything is predictable:

"In this state of languor into which man is bound to fall through the inevitable course of things, the only hope in ten or twelve generations may be a deluge which plunges everything in ignorance again. Then new races will start to go through the same cycle, in which we are perhaps farther advanced than we think" (p. 44).

"Men who have become indifferent through the number and easy availability of pleasures are no longer capable of any kind of interest. They know that ambition is vain, they are sated with the pleasures of love; discernment and delicacy have made them difficult to please in art, intellect, manners, and books; they crave the singular and the extraordinary. If their souls still have any life left in them, the novelty of misfortune might be the only thing that could cure them of their apathy. People who are bored end by looking down on everything, scorning fame, and perhaps scorning scorn itself. They have made a hasty tour of the world they inhabit, and can give you an exact description of it, including the price of everything" (pp. 196–97).

J. H. Jacobi, in his *Woldemar*, expressed a similar sentiment: "The present state of society offers me nothing but the likeness of a dead and stagnant sea, and that is why I should like there to be some deluge, even it were a flood of Barbarians, to sweep away these foul marshes and uncover virgin soil" (2 vols. [Paris, an IV], 1:154–55).

A still keener sense of emptiness and universal absurdity is expressed in the young Benjamin Constant's correspondence with Mme de Charrière: "I feel more than ever the emptiness of everything, how much everything promises while nothing is given, how greatly our strength is above what we are destined to, and how unhappy we must be because of this disproportion. This thought, which I find apt, is not my own; it was formulated by a Piedmontese, a man of wit whom I met at The Hague, a knight of Revel and envoy of Sardinia. He argues that God, i.e., the maker of us and all that surrounds us, died before completing his work; that he had the finest and most grandiose plans and the means to carry them out; that he started to use some of these means, as one puts up scaffolding in order to build a house, and that in the middle of his work he died; that everything that exists now was made for a purpose that exists no longer, and that we in particular feel ourselves destined for something we know nothing about; we are like watches without a dial, whose works are endowed with intelligence and must go on functioning until they are worn out, without knowing why and always saying to themselves: 'I must have a purpose because I go on working'" (June 4, 1790). See Gustave Rudler, *La Jeunesse de Benjamin Constant* (Paris, 1909), pp. 376–77; and Georges Poulet, *Benjamin Constant* (Paris, 1968).

VENICE AT SUNSET

1. Caricature attained particular heights of virtuosity around the year 1789. It was the "hyperrealist" answer to the "hyperidealist" longing to attain the calm realms of the Beautiful.

Caricature, of which Hogarth was the chief great eighteenth-century exponent, played exactly the same critical role as we see played in literature by the *roman bourgeois*, emphasized sometimes to the point of vulgarity in coarseness and parody.

The "noble" types of literature—epic, idyll, and tragedy—were very roughly handled. Fielding's *Tom Thumb* was one of the most virulent examples of mock-tragedy.

Caricature, being hyperrealist, is necessarily hyperexpressive. The dictionaries of the caricaturists were books on physiognomy and the expression of the passions (e.g., the works of Lebrun and Lavater).

So it is not surprising that the neoclassical age, by a sort of inevitable compensation, was the golden age of caricature. It restored the balance. Exaggeratedly atemporal beauties were contrasted with the outrageous uglinesses of the present. Flaxman's England is also the England of James Gillray, a devastating satirist. The aesthetic modes of high society—the neo-Gothic, the romantic picturesque, exotic masquerade—were swifly debunked by the heavy bourgeois vitality of an artist like Rowlandson. We can see this if we glance at the trivial passersby in his watercolor of Strawberry Hill, the house that Horace Walpole tried to render poetic with borrowings from the Gothic (fig. 67).

Caricature, being destructive, was a political weapon. David himself was aware of this, and at the instigation of Marat turned to caricature when the struggle for the Jacobin ideal was in difficulties.

Mozart by Night

1. In the 1770s and 1780s there was a widespread literary fashion for folly or madness and for those ladies who were "*folles intéressantes*," crazy but interesting. A love of excess was evident in many artistic productions, but it almost at once endeavored to cancel itself out by an ostentatious display of sensibility and

67) THOMAS ROWLANDSON (1756–1827).
Exterior View of Strawberry Hill.
(London, Victoria and Albert Museum)

virtue. It is worth noting that music was then considered a propitious medium for folly to manifest itself in to an extreme degree. Music offered marvelous scope for the unrealistic. The usually sober Quatremère de Quincy said as much in a *Dissertation sur les opéras bouffes italiens* in 1789. What did he have in mind? First of all, Pergolesi's *Serva Padrona*, but also more recent examples by Paisiello, Paër and Cimarosa:

"Music is a purely ideal art, in which the model is imaginary and the imitation intellectual. Whether, by means of imitative harmony and the combining of sounds, it succeeds in expressing and reproducing the aural effects of nature, such as winds, storms, the rush of waves, and so on; or whether, by means of an even more ingenious transposition, through the sound of instruments and voices, it expresses the passions and impulses of the soul, borrowing accents from sorrow and joy, making even silence speak and rendering audible the spirit's most unspeakable expression; in any of these cases, the art of music is but a conjuring trick, its model a ghost and its imitation a magic. All it needs are images to paint and passions to express. Applied to theater, it rejects all the subtle transitions differentiating characters, all the refinements of verisimilitude, all the fine arguments, all the concatenation of varied interests, in short all the rational artifice in which dramatic plausibility consists. What it requires are exaggerated ways of behaving and violent contrasts; its least affections are passions, its passions frenzies. It always offers madness for joy, despair for unhappiness, stupefaction for astonishment, rage for anger, vacuousness for naiveté, ecstasy for love, fury for jealousy, and so on. The strings of its lyre are tuned too high to harmonize with any other; its brushes are dipped in colors too strong to combine with the subtle nuances of drama. Drama's model is man as he is; that of music is man as he might be. The limits of drama are the improbable; the limits of music are the impossible" (pp. 19–21).

2. Pierre Jean Jouve, *Le Don Juan de Mozart*, new ed. (Paris, 1968), p. 75.

3. The hypothesis of a Masonic plot, hatched by the duc d'Orléans and his party, has often been put forward to explain the events of 1789. As J. Godechot says in *La Prise de la Bastille* (Paris, 1965): "There is a whole literature, still far from dead, which ascribes the responsibility for the Revolution, and in particular the fateful days of 1789, to the duc d'Orléans. He is said to have been responsible for the riots of New Year's Eve and July 14, for the night of August 4, and for the events in October. The duke certainly tried to turn these happenings to advantage, but it seems very unlikely that he originated them. In any case, if he did play his own game, his efforts were only a tiny addition to

the infinitely greater forces driving Paris, France, and the whole western Europe towards the Revolution" (p. 183).

It is nevertheless true that around 1789 some of the bourgeoisie and the aristocracy were enthusiastic about certain new "systems," preferably those containing elements of mystery and initiation. The success of Cagliostro and Mesmer is one sign of this, among many others. But the "illuminati" and the "initiates" were not all revolutionaries: We have only to remember Cazotte, who was an ardent defender of the monarchy as well as a theorist on will.

I take the following description of the "intellectual" fashions of Paris from *L'Antimagnétisme* (1784), by J. J. Paulet, a doctor: "A man endowed with some genius but given to fanaticism and the spirit of party formed, in silence and in a corner of the Court, a sect which sent down deep roots. I refer to Quesnay and the economists. Their mysterious associations, their inspired tones, their language, the spirit of allegory, some researches into antiquity carried out in our own century, and the lack of principles and real knowledge—all these ushered in a taste for the mystical and spagyric sciences and all that in general is obscure and hidden. There are societies in Paris where enormous sums of money are spent on these sciences. People believe that nature contains powers, invisible spirits, sylphs, which may be at man's disposal; that most natural phenomena and all our own actions spring from hidden sources and from an order of unknown beings; that people have not paid enough attention to talismans, judicial astrology and the magical sciences; that fate and even individual destinies are determined by the guardian spirits who guide us without our knowledge, without our seeing the threads that bind us; in short, that all of us in this world are really like puppets, ignorant and utterly blind slaves. They impress on all minds that it is time to wake up, that man should enjoy his rights, throw off the yoke of invisible powers, or at least discern the hand that guides it.

"This enthusiasm for what is mystical, veiled, and allegorical has become general in Paris and is shared by all those who are well-to-do. People talk of nothing but secret societies. Schools, clubs, museums, music societies, and so on are just so many shrines where people are concerned with nothing but the abstract sciences. The books most sought after are those about secret knowledge, all those which deal with the philosopher's stone and the mystical and cabalistic sciences. But at the moment animal magnetism, taking all in all, is the most fashionable toy, and the one that agitates most minds" (pp. 3–5).

On the part played by "Egyptian mysteries," and in particular the myth of Isis, in revolutionary ceremonial, see Jurgis Baltrusaitis's excellent *La Quête d'Isis* (Paris, 1967).

4. The year 1789 marks the apogee of sonata form and of the classical symphony. It was in 1788 that Mozart finished or had performed his last symphonies: E flat (K. 543); G minor (K. 550); C major (The "Jupiter," K. 551); in 1789 came the marvelous Clarinet Concerto in A major (K. 581). Joseph Haydn, who wrote the "Oxford" Symphony in 1788, went to England in 1790, where his twelve "London Symphonies" had an enormous success. On May 6, 1789, the day after the opening of the States General, the *Mercure de France* reported that "the king's orchestra performed, during his Majesty's levée, a symphony by Haydn, conducted by Monsieur Giroust, superintendant of the king's music." Gossec, born in 1734, was the main French exponent of the symphony at its height.

New operas were appearing all over Europe. In Paris, Dalayrac produced *Les deux petits Savoyards* and *Raoul, sire de Créqui*; Grétry put on *Raoul Barbe-Bleue*, a comedy in prose interspersed with ariettas. Two new works by Paisiello were presented in Caserta and Naples: *Nina o sia la Pazza per Amore* and *I Zingari in Fiera*. Cimarosa, who was in St. Petersburg, produced *La Vergine del Sole* (his greatest success, *Il Matrimonio Segreto*, was first seen in Vienna in 1792). Wieland's *Oberon* inspired two libretti, which were set to music by Wranitsky and Kunzen (Copenhagen). There were also works by Dittersdorf, J. C. Vogel, Lemoyne, Anfossi, and others. Among the operas produced in 1790 was Henri Berton's *Les Rigueurs du Cloître*, thought to be the first opera to take a dramatic liberation as its subject, a theme which remained in fashion until 1820. The highest peak of this genre (*Rettungsoper*, or rescue opera) was reached in Beethoven's *Fidelio* (1805–14).

The year 1789 did not yet see any great national festivities. Julien Tiersot, in *Les Fêtes et les chants de la Révolution française* (Paris, 1908), writes that on August 6 of that year the artists of the Royal Academy of Music sang Gossec's *Requiem* in the district of Saint-Martin-des-Champs "for the repose of the citizens who died in the defense of the common cause." In September the musicians of the National Guard played some of the same composer's military symphonies. It was he who was in charge of the music for the first truly national festivities. His compositions were usually settings of occasional verses by Marie-Joseph Chénier. Gossec had a feeling for great masses of sound (his *Marche lugubre* for Mirabeau's funeral made use of tam-tams). Méhul, born in 1763, was no less ambitious in his orchestrations and massive effects, and also had a lively gift for melody: His fine *Chant du départ*, written in 1794, also to words by M.-J. Chénier, is still impressive when performed in the original version for soloists, choir, and orchestra.

Pierre Jean Jouve (in "Chants de la liberté," *Défense et Illustration* [Neuchâtel, 1943]) describes the impression made nowadays by the musical productions of the Revolution:

"The *Marche lugubre* (for Mirabeau's funeral) has an austere grandeur, in wood and steel, with its terrible naked drums, and produces a sort of aural abyss with the basses which make it a typical example of the style. We may compare it in our minds with David's *Marat assassiné*. We seem to see the same cruelty of the bath with its blood-tinged water, of the green rug, the sinister wooden case, and the corpse suddenly become smiling and spiritual, 'the divine Marat'; there is the same absence of shadow, the same august harshness and sense of darkness. These contradictory forces are united by the metaphysics of antique Fate, which drapes and expresses suffering through an excess of painful harmony. The *Marche lugubre*, which sometimes surpasses in intensity Beethoven's famous *Marche funèbre*, should be the expression of national mourning."

We should not forget that for its ceremonial the Revolution also made use of works composed without any patriotic intention. Vogel, a German composer who died in Paris in 1788, had written an opera based on a libretto from Metastasio and called *Démophoon*. The opera was produced in 1789. The severe and yet sweeping overture was often performed at patriotic ceremonies, and in particular in September 1790 "for the funeral of the officers killed at Nancy" (J. Tiersot, pp. 48–49). In his *Offrande à la liberté* (1792), Gossec combined his own superb orchestration of Rouget de Lisle's *Marseillaise* (composed, like the *Chant de guerre de l'armée du Rhin*, in 1792) with an adaptation of an air from Dalayrac's comic opera *Renaud d'Ast*, composed before the Revolution and first performed in 1787. Thus the serenade, *"Vous qui d'amoureuse aventure Courez et plaisirs et dangers"* ("You who court the pleasures and dangers of amorous adventure") became *"Veillons au salut de l'empire, Veillons au maintien de nos droits"* ("Let us fight for the well-being of the empire and the safeguarding of our rights").

THE SOLAR MYTH OF THE REVOLUTION

1. Needless to say, this replaced the solar myth of the monarchy, just as the philosophy of the Enlightenment used for its

own purposes the images connected with the theology of light.

Historians since Tocqueville have known that the central-ized administration of the Ancien Régime tended to promote uniformity in law throughout all France and to favor the equality of subjects before the law. It still remained to transform subjects into free citizens, and this was the achievement of the Revo-lution.

2. Rabaut Saint-Etienne, p. 83.

3. Blake, *The French Revolution*, Pages 3–4, in *The Poetry and Prose of William Blake*, ed. David V. Erdman, Commentary by Harold Bloom (Garden City, N.Y., 1970), p. 285.

4. On the details of that day, see Jacques Godechot's recent book *La Prise de la Bastille* (Paris, 1965). We should remember the symbolic uses to which the remains of the fortress were put and out of which the entrepreneur Palloy made a very lucrative business: Some of the stones were used to finish the Pont Louis-XVI, built according to the plans of the architect Perronet, and later known as the Pont de la Révolution and later the Pont de la Concorde; other stones "were carved so as to reproduce a relief model of the fortress" and sent to the provinces (Godechot, p. 322).

It is appropriate here to recall the memories and reflections in Book 5 of Chateaubriand's *Mémoires d'Outre-tombe*: "The experts hastened to perform an autopsy of the Bastille. Tempo-rary cafés were set up in tents; people flocked there as to the Foire Saint-Germain or Longchamp; numerous carriages drove by or stopped under the towers, whose stones were being thrown down in swirls of dust. Elegantly dressed women, young men of fashion, standing at different levels of the Gothic rubble, mingled with half-naked workmen demolishing the walls to the acclamations of the crowd. It was a rendezvous for the most famous orators, the best-known men of letters, the most cele-brated painters, the most popular actors and actresses, the most fashionable dancers, the most illustrious foreigners, the lords of the Court, and the ambassadors of Europe; the old France had come there to end, the new had come there to begin.

"No matter how wretched or odious in itself, no event should be taken lightly if its circumstances are serious and if it marks an era: What we should see in the taking of the Bastille (and what people did not see at the time) is not a violent act for the emancipation of a people, but emancipation itself, the real result of that act.

"People admired what they should have condemned—that which was accidental. And they did not look toward the future for the accomplished fate of a whole people, for changes in manners, ideas, political authority, or a renewal of the human race, all of which was opened up by the taking of the Bastille, a sort of bloody jubilee. Brute anger produced ruins, but beneath this anger lurked the intelligence that laid down among the ruins the foundations of a new edifice."

5. Tocqueville, *L'Ancien Régime et la Révolution*, 2 vols. (Paris, 1953), 2:131.

6. Johann Gottlieb Fichte, *Beitrag zur Berichtigung des Urteils des Publikums über die französische Revolution*, in *Staatsphilosophische Schriften* (Leipzig: Meiner, 1919), p. 3.

7. For many people living at the time, the return to principles seemed to herald a new era: Rigorous knowledge, and action based on it, was supplanting a now outmoded age of imagination, invention, and fruitfulness in the arts. (In politics, what was really beginning was not so much the age of knowledge as the age of ideologies.) We may quote some characteristic lines from J.-P. Rabaut Saint-Etienne: "It is part of the natural progress of the human mind that the age of philosophy should necessarily succeed the age of the fine arts. We begin by imitating nature, and end by studying it; we first observe objects, and then search for their causes and principles. Under Louis XV, men of letters became different; and at a time when poetry,

architecture, painting, and sculpture had produced many masterpieces and when novelty, which had lent such value to the fine arts, was exhausted and great conceptions grown more difficult, men's minds turned naturally toward the search for principles themselves. The century of the reason which examines succeeded that of the imagination which paints" (pp. 24–25).

8. Fichte, *Zurückforderung der Denkfreiheit von den Fürsten Europens, die sie bisher unterdrückten*, in *Werke, 1791–1794*, ed. Reinhard Lauth and Hans Jacob (Stuttgart–Bad Cannstatt: Friedrich Fromann Verlag, 1964), 1:opposite 166.

9. The first edition of Lagrange's *Mécanique analytique* appeared in 1788. Laplace published his *Théorie du mouvement et de la figure elliptique des planètes* in 1784, his *Exposition du système du monde* in 1796, and his *Mécanique céleste* in 1799.

With Lagrange, classical mechanics was unified and expressed in terms of mathematics. Lagrange's intentions are set out in his *Advertisement*. They were:

"To reduce mechanical theory and problem-solving to general formulae, the natural development of which give all the equations necessary for the solution of every problem."

To bring together and present "from a single point of view the various Principles discovered so far to facilitate the solving of mechanical questions, showing their mutual dependence and making it possible to assess their correctness and scope."

" . . . There are no Diagrams in this book. The methods I am expounding require neither constructions nor arguments, whether geometrical or mechanical, but only algebraic operations regularly and uniformly carried out. Those who love Analysis will be pleased to see Mechanics emerge as a new branch of it, and will thank me for having extended its scope in this way."

Ernst Mach, analyzing the ambitions of classical mechanics at the end of the nineteenth century, wrote: "When we see how the encyclopedists of the eighteenth century thought themselves close to their goal, which was the physico-mechanical explanation of the whole of nature; and how Laplace imagined a genius who could describe the state of the universe at a given moment in the future, if, to start off with, he knew all the masses it was composed of, together with their positions and velocities; then not only does this enthusiastic overestimate of the value of eighteenth-century notions of physics and mechanics seem very excusable, but it also presents a spectacle that is reassuring, noble, and elevated, and we can sympathize from the bottom of our hearts with an intellectual delight unique in history.

"Now that a century has gone by and we have had more time to think about it, the encyclopedists' conception of the world strikes us as a *mechanical mythology* as distinct from the animistic mythology of the ancient religions. Both contain imaginary and unjustified amplifications of a unilateral knowledge" (*La Mécanique, exposé historique et critique de son développement*, French trans. by Emile Bertrand [Paris, 1904], p. 433).

10. Tocqueville, 1:89.

Principles and Will

1. "We are approaching a state of crisis and the age of revolutions. . . . I think it is impossible for the great monarchies of Europe to last much longer." This prophecy, uttered by Rousseau in 1762 in *Emile*, resembles many other prophecies in projecting on the future an image of the past. Rousseau had read Plutarch, Livy, and Machiavelli, had attempted to write a *Lucretia*, and had thought a lot about the expulsion of the Tarquins: From all this he had retained the archetypical image of a repub-

lican Revolution which, banishing tyranny and rejecting both despotism and the impurity of unbridled desire, would usher in the reign of virtue and chastity. Rousseau also knew the works of Locke, Algernon Sidney, and the classical theorists of natural law, and was familiar with the principles that had triumphed in England at the time of the 1688 Revolution. While he was still adolescent, Geneva had presented him with the painful spectacle of civil war.

Was Rousseau urging struggle and hope? Did he see the fall of the monarchies as the sign of an age of justice? Unlike Turgot and the theorists of progress, Rousseau was not inclined to trust in history and "enlightenment." He did not expect philosophy to bring about public well-being. He was more apt to predict catastrophe: The defects of civilization and the interaction of aggravated self-interest and pride would drive Europe into bloody anarchy; the world would be shaken by "short and frequent revolutions"; history had almost reached its end, which was just as savage as its beginning; and the violence of this sunset would bring back the "war of all against all" that according to Hobbes had preceded the birth of society. By becoming civilized by the methods of inequality, which are the methods of sin, man had condemned himself to death. Was it still possible to regenerate society itself? It was probably too late. When he wrote *Emile*, when he took refuge in reverie, Rousseau seemed to have given up hoping for anything more than a respite for the individual. At a crucial moment in which the human mind was discovering the reality of history and its own link with the historical moment, it was almost simultaneously tempted to find its salvation, not in and through history, but apart from it, and almost in contempt of its hitherto inevitable constraint. One whole aspect of Rousseau's work offers his contemporaries a pessimistic reading of history, and the prospect of finding refuge in the solitude of personal existence. This part of Rousseau's writings, though it is not the whole, acted as a guide to superior souls horrified by the

[247]

way the world was going and seeking happiness in a secret belief in their own innocence. The state of crisis and the age of revolutions were, for the individual, a schism which threw him back on his own autonomy, his difference, and his painful survival in a universe inhabited by death.

But Rousseau did not utterly accept the failure of history. He continued to formulate the norms of a legitimate social life, even though at first these norms were nowhere likely to be put into practice. He became a writer in order that men, too long under the spell of lies and iniquity, should waken into consciousness of their misfortune; so that oppressed nations might at last see that instead of being bound together by true social bonds they wore the chains of slavery. Rousseau, citizen of Geneva, spoke to them in order to break the spell, to help them recognize the yoke of bondage beneath the "garlands of flowers" that concealed it. The imminent catastrophe predicted by Rousseau might be only the dark background to a miraculous event. The presaged disaster acted as a foil to the frail image of a last chance: By a general burst of energy, or better still under the leadership of an inspired lawgiver, societies might return to their true principles—liberty, equality, and civic virtue. Rousseau's emotional eloquence made his age seem the arena of a great alternative: to yield to the fatal fascination of corruption or to be born again to a new vigor, a rough and sober simplicity. Rousseau's language, haunted by the idea of sin, was a culpabilizing language: It accused his contemporaries, it gave them warning. It issued a summons presented as a last chance: If luxury, vanity, despotism, and servitude were allowed to grow worse, all would end in blood. Salvation, if it could still be hoped for, could only be the result of undeserved grace. But so strong was the need for salvation and so vivid his horror of chaos that Rousseau continued to argue, in the face of his own doubts and the strong assertions of his own historical pessimism, in favor of the precarious theory of a "return to legitimate institutions" and a rebirth of the social body. It would be a rebirth through crisis; a regeneration and palingenesis offered to those who would drink the "water of oblivion." After the long feverish night in which all was confusion, men might awaken to the light of a genuine new beginning. "As certain maladies upset men's minds and take from them the memory of the past, so sometimes in the lifetime of States there may be violent periods when revolutions affect nations as certain attacks of illness affect individuals, when horror of the past takes the place of oblivion, and the State, consumed by civil war, rises so to speak from its own ashes, emerging from the arms of death to find again the vigor of its youth" (*Contrat social*, 2:vii).

Admittedly, this was not a program for action or a plan for reform. In a way it was more: a mythical image of life rediscovered through the ordeal of death; of the crossing of a threshold, the abolition of the past, a glorious resurrection. Rousseau made use of the images theology had employed to depict the Day of Judgment: He offered a lay version, a Judgment which would take place not in the Kingdom of God but in human history.

Rousseau did not create these ideas and images out of his own head. He found them scattered about the world in which he lived. But it was he who gave them the vehement form and imperious tone that made them effective. His age, which admired him to the point of idolatry, was only seeing itself in him. Rousseau's preaching certainly did not "cause" the French Revolution, but it did help the men of 1789 to see their situation as a revolutionary crisis. What Rousseau (and the philosophers) said, though it did not determine events, created the feeling that gave events their exalted significance. It developed the concepts which political thought and action were to put to the test, and it also gave life to the great mythical images to which the collective imagination was to become attached. It offered a language in which the Revolution, solemnly and not always understanding itself, could glorify itself in oaths, feasts, cults, and celebrations.

I would have preferred not to omit either Voltaire or the Encyclopedists, but since we are primarily concerned with the images of 1789 I felt I must give his full due to the man who dominated the life of the imagination of his age.

For Rousseauism both before and during the Revolution, see the works of André Monglond, and in particular his *Histoire intérieure du Préromantisme français*, 2 vols. (Grenoble, 1930). See also Pierre Trahard, *La Sensibilité révolutionnaire (1789– 1794)* (Paris, 1936).

Daniel Mornet's systematic survey in his *Origines intellectuelles de la Révolution française* (Paris, 1933) enables us to define the respective roles of "intellect" and circumstance: "Certainly, if the Ancien Régime had been threatened by nothing else but intellect, it would have been in no danger. In order to act, this intellect needed a springboard—the sufferings of the people, political unease. But these political causes would probably not have been enough to bring about the Revolution, or at least to bring it about so rapidly. It was intellect that discerned and organized the consequences involved and gradually insisted on the States General. And from the States General, though intellect did not suspect it, was to come the Revolution" (p. 477).

By way of illustration, two facts about Rousseau. After an interruption due to the events of July 1789, the Opéra opened again with a performance of Rousseau's *Devin du Village*, for the benefit of the families of the rioters who had fallen in the attack on the Bastille. And on the recommendation of Lakanal, dated September 15, 1794 (29 fructidor, an II), the Convention adopted a bill for transferring Rousseau's remains from Ermenonville to the Panthéon. Here is a significant passage from Lakanal's speech: "The *Contrat social* seems to have been written to be read in the presence of the assembled human race, to teach it what it has been and what it has lost. . . . But the great maxims expounded in the *Contrat social*, self-evident and simple as they seem to us today, had little effect at the time. People did not pay them sufficient attention either to fear or to profit by them. They were too far above men's heads, even of those who were or thought themselves superior to the common herd. In a way it was the Revolution which explained the *Contrat social* to us" (quoted in J.-M. Paris, *Honneurs publics rendus à la mémoire de J.-J. Rousseau, étude historique* [Geneva, 1878]).

2. Rabaut Saint-Etienne, p. 141.

3. *Anniversaire du 21 janvier*, by Citoyen Lebrun, in *Recueil des chants philosophiques, civiques et moraux* (Paris, an VII [1798–99]), pp. 114–15.

4. Here we should recall the attitude consistently adopted by J.-P. Marat, who put his readers on their guard about the rhetoric of generosity and the civic ceremonial of the "early revolution." After the night of August 4, 1789, when the privileged orders solemnly renounced their social advantages, Marat wrote in *L'Ami du Peuple*: "One is tempted to suspect that the confidence and integrity of the Deputies of the Third Estate have been affected by the influence of politics, hidden beneath the mask of patriotism." In his view, the true causes of the night of August 4 were to be sought in the violent anger of the peasant masses, not in the spontaneous will of the privileged:

"No doubt acts of justice and benevolence inspired by humanity and patriotic love impatient to make itself known were bound to fill the onlookers with admiration, and in these efforts of generosity to outdo itself, enthusiasm was bound to border on transport. But was this really what happened? Far be it from me to outrage virtue, but we should not let ourselves be duped by anyone. If it was benevolence that inspired these sacrifices, we must admit it was rather slow in making itself heard. Come! It was in the light of the flames of their burning châteaus that they found the magnanimity to renounce the privilege of keeping in chains men who got back their freedom by armed struggle! It was the sight of the sufferings of despoilers, peculators, and satellites of despotism that gave them the generosity to renounce seigneurial tithes and no longer demand anything from wretches who have difficulty in getting enough to eat!" (*L'Ami du Peuple*, nos. 11 and 12, September 21 and 23, 1789).

Karl Marx, at the beginning of his book on the Dix-huit Brumaire of Louis Bonaparte, referred to the fashion for Roman costume which in fact preceded the advent of a bourgeois society. But Marat's cult of the heart gives rise to similar reflections concerning a social stratum other than the bourgeoisie.

THE GEOMETRICAL CITY

1. Not everyone was carried away by the drama of the Revolution. There were many that stood aside, and they should not be neglected.

The Goncourts, among others, were very interested in these exceptions, and we can read, perhaps with some irritation, the vignettes they drew of them in the style of Boilly or Debucourt in their *Histoire de la Société française pendant la Révolution* and *Histoire de la Société française pendant le Directoire*. So long as we do not lose sight of the major events and interests involved, it can be useful to consider the Revolution in its minor historical aspects, those relating to cafes, theaters, places of fashionable resort, prostitution, songs, and caricature. It is not irrelevant that the sentimental, or *larmoyant*, writings that were popular before the Revolution retained their audience under the Terror. In her *Considérations sur la Révolution française*, Mme de Staël reminds us: "While the executions were taking place, the theaters were full as usual; novels were published with titles like

Nouveau voyage sentimental, *L'Amitié dangereuse*, and *Ursule et Sophie*; in short, all the insipidity and frivolity of life survived side by side with its darkest furies." Comedy, with Collin d'Harleville; genre painting (which often took the form of street scenes), with Boilly; licentious engravings, with Debucourt—all these were still produced, suggesting an almost unbroken continuity between the bagatelles of the Ancien Régime and the diversions of the Empire.

Variations in the female image were very marked. The craze for the antique freed women from the corsets and whalebones that had hitherto imprisoned them. The tight waist disappeared. Light, flimsy gowns imitated the draperies of the Greek chlamys. Hair was shorter or arranged more freely. One modification was very important: The slight eroticism of the eighteenth century had rarely been vulgar, whereas, with the Empire, frivolity, even "Parisian" frivolity, came to bear the indelible marks of vulgarity. (The word *vulgarité* was a neologism which Mme de Staël made use of in 1800 in her book on *La Littérature* to stigmatize the falling off in literary taste that took place in the course of the Revolution.)

Henry Harrisse's *L. L. Boilly, peintre, dessinateur et lithographe, 1761–1845* (Paris, 1898), is still the most complete study of this artist, with his quick eye and superficial verve. For Debucourt see M. Fenaille, *L'Œuvre gravée de Debucourt* (Paris, 1899).

2. "Wishing to give encouragement to artists who through lack of commissions were turning to counterrevolution, the Convention on August 14, 1793, decreed a competition in architecture to be open and available to all, but in accordance with the desire expressed by the architect Dufourny the entries were to be 'as simple as virtue itself.' Architecture, he added, should be regenerated through geometry" (Spire Blondel, *L'Art pendant la Révolution* [Paris, n.d.], pp. 86–87).

3. Fichte, *Zurückforderung der Denkfreiheit*, in *Staatsphilosophische Schriften*, pp. 5–6.

4. Joseph Joubert, *Pensées*, selected and introduced by Georges Poulet (Paris, 1966), p. 221.

5. C.-N. Ledoux, *L'Architecture* . . . (Paris, 1804), quoted by J. C. Lemagny in "Les Architectes visionnaires de la fin du XVIIIe siècle" (Catalogue de l'exposition du Cabinet des Estampes, Geneva, 1965).

6. Ledoux, p. 14.

7. The new architecture wanted to be *true*. The theorists of rococo, on the other hand, had found merit in a "fine untruth." Emil Kaufmann has recalled Algarotti's revealing phrase: "*Dal vero più bella è la menzogna.*" "Taking up a position radically opposed to that of Lodoli, he declared that structure could not be beautiful in itself: What made it beautiful was ornament" (*L'Architecture au siècle des Lumières*, French trans. by O. Bernier [Paris, 1963], p. 112). Kaufmann's book describes the part played by Lodoli in defining the new "functionalist" theory of architecture.

For enlightened amateurs in 1789, the work of Palladio was the unsurpassable model in architecture. In Goethe's view, Palladio's achievement consisted in the harmonious fusion of decorative untruth (columns and colonnades) with functional truth (walls). When he arrived in Vicenza on September 19, 1786, Goethe hastened to see the buildings there by Palladio. "He is a great man inwardly; and his grandeur comes from his inwardness to be expressed externally. The worst difficulty he, like all modern architects, had to deal with, was the skillful use of colonnades in civil architecture; for to combine columns and walls is always a contradiction. But how he succeeded, by hard work, in combining them! How he impresses us with the presence of his works and makes us forget his skill in persuasion! There is something divine in his buildings: It is the exact equivalent of the form created by a great poet, who out of both truth and untruth composes a third reality whose thus borrowed existence exercises a magical power over us" (*Italian Journey*).

Quatremère de Quincy in his turn praised Palladio as a living example of synthesis and the middle way: "Palladio's style has a propriety which should cause it to be followed widely; it is . . . a kind of middle way between the systematic austerity which some exclusive spirits misuse in their imitation of the antique and the anarchical and licentious doctrines of those who reject all system because none can be universally applied. . . . Palladio's buildings have a reason that is always clear, a simplicity of development, *a satisfying harmony between the laws of necessity and those of pleasure*; such a harmony, indeed, that it is impossible to say which took precedence. . . . So it is true to say that Palladio has become the master most universally followed in all Europe, and, so to speak, the legislator of the Moderns" (*Encyclopédie méthodique, Architecture*, s.v. "Palladio"). This was true of the young United States of America as well as Europe. In 1787 Jefferson's plans for the Capitol in Richmond were based on Palladio and the *Maison carrée* in Nîmes.

8. Quatremère de Quincy, who advocated a simplicity "not reduced mathematically to the lowest common factor," distinguished three aspects of this quality: "Simplicity of conception in the general plan of a building. Simplicity in the intended general effect. Simplicity in the means by which the plan is carried out.

"It is above all the nature and purpose of the building which should inspire in the architect the general notion which is to serve as a type for his invention; for with every building the use to which it is to be put should give a simple basic datum which becomes the primary guideline in its composition. Whatever diversity and multiplicity of detail may be suggested in the plan, it will always have the merit of simplicity if the artist has been able to subordinate all the parts to one general motif which so to speak contains its explanation" (*Encyclopédie méthodique, Architecture*, s.v. "Simplicité").

9. Ledoux, p. 17.

10. Quatremère de Quincy, *Encyclopédie méthodique, Architecture*, s.v. "Bizarrerie."

11. Ibid., s.v. "Grandeur."

12. Ibid.

13. Etienne-Louis Boullée, *Essai sur l'Art*, (Paris, 1968), pp. 132–37.

14. The spherical form constantly used by "visionary" architects was no longer the symbol, as it had been in the Renaissance, of a closed universe. In Laplace's *Mécanique céleste*, space was infinite. The image of the sphere could only correspond to the solar system. Soon, as voluntarism grew more and more widespread, the image would come to be used chiefly in the field of individual psychology, in which voluntary being is seen as *concentrated* being. Here it is worth consulting the pages devoted to the romantic era in Georges Poulet's *Les Métamorphoses du cercle* (Paris, 1961).

According to one "illuminatus," Louis-Claude de Saint-Martin, the idea of an individual center was linked to that of a cosmic and spiritual center which was the source of life. His *Homme de Désir* (1790) presents a grand vision of universal harmony and correspondence—undoubtedly one of the "hidden sources" of romanticism:

"I marveled at how this universal source animated all beings and imparted to each the unquenchable fire from which all derive their motion. Each individual formed a center in which were reflected all the points of its individual sphere.

"These individuals were themselves only the points of the particular spheres which made up their class and species, and which were also governed by a center.

"These spheres in turn had their centers in the different kingdoms of nature, and these kingdoms had their centers in the great regions of the universe.

"These great regions corresponded to active centers endowed with inextinguishable life, and these centers had as their center the primal and unique driving force of all that is.

"Thus all is individual, and yet all is one. What then is this great Being which from its impenetrable centre sees all beings, all stars and the whole universe forming but one point on its incommensurable sphere?

" . . . I heard all the parts of the universe form one sublime melody in which high sounds were balanced by low and the sounds of desire by those of pleasure and joy. They aided each other so that order might be established everywhere and herald the great unity itself.

" . . . It was not as it is in our dark abode, where sounds may be compared only with sounds and colors with colors, one substance only with a similar substance; there all was one.

"Light echoed sound, melody gave birth to light, colors had motion, because the colors were living and objects were at once audible, translucent, and mobile enough to interpenetrate and cover the whole of space in one sweep.

"In the midst of this magnificent spectacle I saw the human soul arise, like a radiant sun emerging from the waves."

15. Emil Kaufmann, "Influences italiennes et romantiques," *L'Architecture au siècle des Lumières*, trans. Olivier Bernier (Paris, 1963), p. 219. In this connection, see Joseph Rykwert, *The First Moderns: The Architects of the Eighteenth Century* (Cambridge, 1980).

Speaking Architecture, Words Made Eternal

1. Quoted by Louis Hautecoeur, *Louis David* (Paris, 1954), p. 290.

Our examination so far has been confined to a few trends (many of them purely speculative) shown by the boldest architects of the day. Needless to say, our picture has not been complete. But the interest we still rightly take in Ledoux, Boullée, Poyet, and Lequeu should not make us forget Cellérier, Bélanger, Gondoin, Gisors, De Wailly, Brongniart, Chalgrin, Victor Louis, etc.; nor the great Italians, like Valadier and Quarenghi, whether they built in their own country or in far-off Russia; nor such Englishmen as John Nash, John Soane, and James Wyatt. It would be dangerous to reduce the architecture of 1789 to one "general spirit": To speak here of ease, dignity, elegance, and regular monumentality would be to say little. Admittedly, there was a common language which lent itself to free and ingenious solutions: One pure grammar seems to govern all plans and all practical realizations alike. But even in the architects whom their contemporaries regarded as "discreet" or sober we discern a liking for strength, a penchant for effects of simple grandeur, a dignity which yet preserves the decorative function, a sometimes strange combination of severe rigor in the main structure with decorative luxury in the interiors: There is a kind of reserve that limits ornament only to intensify its effect. Rigid fluting establishes a contrasting dialogue with sinuous forms inherited from an earlier age; decorative arabesque tends to sacrifice its many ramifications so as to obey a deeper symmetry. Foliated scrolls have more stereotyped and obsessional motifs; their frivolity is haunted by the memory of Pompeii, Palmyra, or Egypt and becomes at once more distant and more abstract. But already exotic or backward-looking fantasies, such as the neo-Gothic constructions of Wyatt, had made their appearance in England.

If I had, for their exemplary value, to mention briefly some works undertaken in 1789, I should choose the Brandenburg Gate, inspired by the Propylaea in Athens, built in Berlin by Karl Langhans (the sculptor Gottfried Schadow was to add the victory quadriga); also the overall plan drawn up by Pierre Charles L'Enfant for the extension of the city of Washington. In both instances what was at stake was the structure and prestige, both real and symbolical, of a capital.

THE OATH: DAVID

1. The only picture David sent to the private view of the 1789 Salon was the *Paris and Helen* he had painted for the comte d'Artois, later Charles X. To this painting, Alexandrian rather than Homeric, was later added a work of Roman inspiration—*Brutus*. Both pictures are overburdened with archaeological reminiscences, but their spirit is strangely different. What predominates in *Paris and Helen* (fig. 68), a work with no internal tension, is femininity; while the basic factor in *Brutus* is manly resolution, in vivid contrast to the helpless consternation of the women's group. Its subject led *Brutus* to be regarded as a criticism of Louis XVI's indulgence toward the members of his family and entourage who opposed the Revolution. Very few works shown in the Salon of 1789 reflected current events. But Hubert Robert showed not only views and ruins but also a sketch from nature of *La Bastille dans les premiers jours de sa démolition*.

By way of contrast it is worth recalling the subjects of some

68) JACQUES-LOUIS DAVID (1748–1825).
The Loves of Paris and Helen. 1789.
(Paris, Musée du Louvre. Photo Musées Nationaux)

of the works shown. M.-J. Vien offered *L'Amour fuyant l'esclavage* (one woman foolishly opens the cage and Love escapes; another woman rushes to recapture it); also *Une mère faisant porter des offrandes à l'autel de Minerve.* F. A. Vincent showed *Zeuxis choisissant pour modèles les plus belles filles de Crotone pour en former l'image de Vénus.* La Grenée the elder was represented by *Alexandre consultant l'oracle d'Apollon*; La Grenée the younger by *Télémaque et Mentor jetés dans l'île de*

Calypso and *Achille sous l'habit de fille, reconnu par Ulysse*; J.-B. Regnault: *Descente de Croix* and *Scène du Déluge*. Joseph Vernet: *Le Naufrage de Virginie*; *Fin d'orage*; and *Pêche au lever du soleil*. Mme Vigée-Lebrun: *Portrait d'Hubert Robert*. Dumont: *Portrait du Roi en miniature*; *Portrait de Vien*; etc.

The *Collection des livrets* of the Salons was reprinted by J. Guiffrey, Paris, 1869–1872, in 42 volumes.

For the antique reminiscences in *Paris and Helen*, see the article by E. Coche de la Ferté and F. Guey, "Analyse archéologique et psychologique d'un tableau de David," *Revue Archéologique* 2 (1950):129–61 (with notes by Charles Picard). Many David drawings after the antique are preserved in the Louvre. See Jean Adhémar, *David: Naissance du génie d'un peintre* (Paris, 1953), in particular pp. 39–45.

2. J.-F. Ducis, who translated Shakespeare very freely for the French stage, composed an *Epître à Vien*, "happy restorer of the French school." Vien's pictures were not the only ones he referred to; he also described famous canvases by his pupils and contemporaries, such as Regnault, Taillasson, and Vincent. Ducis spoke at length of David, mentioning one after the other the *Horaces*, *Brutus*, and the *Sabines* (1799). Here is his description of *Brutus*:

> "O Brutus! what spectacle is preparing itself for your eyes!
> I see two bloody corpses, but I cannot see their faces.
> What! Your sons are no more! Unhappy father!
> Who ordered this disastrous death?
> You yourself: but alas, Rome had to be held dearer:
> You could not at once be consul and father.
> You sit there motionless, averting your eyes,
> Beside an altar, seeking support from your gods.
> Death is in your heart; but heavens! with what charms,
> So lovely in their innocence, youth and tears,
> Your daughters tell you of their artless sorrow. . . .

By weeping not, you make me weep.
Brutus sheds no tear; he suffers, and this great man
Offers thanks to the gods after having saved Rome.
But David, you must not weary in your ardour,
But rival and surpass yourself.
When your art inspires you and calls you to glory,
It is instinct that speaks, and in it you must believe.
What can genius not do! It does as it wills:
Its secret is often unknown to itself.
Our work is art; but instinct is genius.
With this creative fire, this very soul of life,
Michelangelo burns, and Tasso is consumed.
This fire which feels, sees, judges, invents, and arranges
Sometimes seems to rest in an apparent calm:
But the volcano only slept; it erupts with a roar,
And out of it rises the masterpiece in splendor."

3. *Tragedie di Vittorio Alfieri*, 4 vols. (Italia, 1820), vol. 4, *Bruto primo*, act 5, scene 2, p. 101.

4. André Chénier, *Œuvres complètes* (Paris, Pléiade, 1940), p. 168.

5. Jean Leymarie, *La Peinture française* (Geneva, 1962), p. 18.

6. Charles Baudelaire, "Le musée classique du bazar Bonne Nouvelle," in *Œuvres complètes*, ed. C. Pichois, 2 vols. (Paris, Pléiade, 1976), 2:409–10.

7. People once used to attribute the restoration of true painting to the timid and correct Joseph-Marie Vien.
"The great man, after making a special study of nature, set before his pupils, as models of beauty, the statues of antiquity and the paintings and cartoons of Raphael, Giulio Romano, and Michelangelo. He had himself accepted the principles of the Italian School, and his work and example provided the students

with a *rule* of which the theory and development aimed at perfection. . . .

"Vien only prepared the way that was subsequently trodden so gloriously by David, and the honest old gentleman agreed that this was so. One day when he honoured me with a visit I spoke of the services he had rendered our country by attempting a new restoration of the art of drawing and painting. He answered modestly: "*I set the door ajar; David threw it open*" (Alexandre Lenoir, *Observations scientifiques et critiques sur le génie* . . . [Paris, 1821], pp. 259–62).

The painting with which Vien was admitted to the Academy was a picture of *Dédale attachant les ailes de son fils Icare.* For us he is the artist who took elements for allegorical scenes in pure "Louis Seize" style from Greek vases, antique bas-reliefs, and the discoveries at Pompeii and Herculaneum. His *Marchande d'amours* was an enormous success. "He painted several pictures with subjects from Homer, but his genius was never able to rise to the height of the poet" (ibid.).

8. David sat in the Convention, voted for the death of the king, supported Robespierre, and was imprisoned after the 9 Thermidor. He contributed toward the abolition of the Academies. On David's role in the Convention, see J. J. Guiffrey, "Louis David, pièces diverses sur le rôle de cet artiste pendant La Révolution," in *Nouvelles Archives de l'Art français* (1872), pp. 414–28; D. L. Dowd, *Pageant Master of the Republic: Jacques-Louis David and the French Revolution* (Lincoln, Neb., 1948); "The French Revolution and the Painters," *French Historical Studies*, 1, no. 2 (1959):127–48; James A. Leith, *The Idea of Art as Propaganda in France*, University of Toronto Romance Series, no. 8, 1965 (this has an excellent bibliography); A. Schnapper, *David, témoin de son temps* (Paris, 1980).

9. Greuze had fallen out with everyone before the Revolution. He had separated from his wife and turned his back on the

Academy, which in 1769 had declined to admit him as a historical painter. After 1785 the public took little interest in him. But he did not stop painting, and during the Revolution "some groups of his pictures were sometimes even presented in the Republican celebrations" (Renouvier). In the years before his death in 1805 he sent a few pictures to the Salon, canvases in his usual sentimental vein (in 1802 he sent *Un Cultivateur remettant la charrue à son fils*). See J. Martin, *Œuvre de J.-B. Greuze*, Catalogue Raisonné (Paris, 1908).

We may suppose that if it had not been for the fall of the monarchy Fragonard's career as an illustrator and decorator would have continued longer. The events of 1789 apparently delayed the publication of his excellent illustrations to La Fontaine's *Contes*. After living for a time in Grasse, he returned to Paris in 1791. It is probable that he collaborated with his sister-in-law, Marguerite Gérard. (See Jacques Wilhelm, "Fragonard eut-il un atelier?" *Médecine de France* 25 [1951]: 1728.) David was kind to him. In 1794 he was a member of the *Jury des arts*, then (together with Vincent, Hubert Robert, Pécault, and Pajou) member of the *Conservatoire du Musée*. But he was forgotten by the public. (See George Wildenstein, *Fragonard* [Phaidon, 1961].)

JOHANN HEINRICH FÜSSLI (FÜSELI)

1. Reynold's fifteenth and last *Discourse* on painting (December 1790) was a eulogy of Michelangelo, who was presented as unsurpassed master of the pictorial art. According to Reynolds, Michelangelo had lifted art to sudden maturity by virtue of his imagination, which Reynolds considered the most sublime

the world had ever seen. In comparison, his followers and imitators were lesser artists.

"At present I shall only observe, that the subordinate parts of our Art, and perhaps the other Arts, expand themselves by a slow and progressive growth; but those which depend on a native vigour of imagination generally burst forth at once in fullness of beauty. Of this Homer probably, and Shakspeare more assuredly, are signal examples. Michael Angelo possessed the poetical part of our art in a most eminent degree; and the same daring spirit, which urged him first to explore the unknown regions of the imagination, delighted with the novelty, and animated by the success of his discoveries, could not have failed to stimulate and impel him forward in his career beyond those limits, which his followers, destitute of the same incentives, had not strength to pass."

"In pursuing this great Art, it must be acknowledged that we labour under greater difficulties than those who were born in the age of its discovery, and whose minds from their infancy were habituated to this style; who learnt it as language, as their mother tongue. They had no mean taste to unlearn; they needed no persuasive discourse to allure them to a favourable reception of it, no abstruse investigation of its principles to convince them of the great latent truths on which it is founded. We are constrained, in these later days, to have recourse to a sort of Grammar and Dictionary, as the only means of recovering a dead language. It was by them learned by rote, and perhaps better learned that way than by precept.

"The style of Michael Angelo, which I have compared to language, and which may, poetically speaking, be called the language of the Gods, now no longer exists, as it did in the fifteenth century" (Sir Joshua Reynolds, *Discourses on Art*, ed. Robert R. Wark, published for the Paul Mellon Centre for Studies in British Art [London] by Yale University Press [New Haven, 1975], p. 278).

Reynolds's own painting showed a reasoned eclecticism and marvelous skill as a colorist. His *Death of Dido* (1789) aims at combining the fascination of Correggio with the color of the Venetians. Edgar Wind has shown that Dido's attitude is taken almost "literally" from that of a *Psyché endormie* depicted by a disciple of Giulio Romano on a ceiling in the Palazzo del Tè. (See Edgar Wind, "Borrowed Attitudes in Reynolds and Hogarth," *Journal of the Warburg and Courtauld Institutes* 2 [1938–39]: 182–85.)

2. Benjamin West and John Singleton Copley, though born in the New World, pursued their careers chiefly in England. West, as we have already seen, became celebrated, and succeeded Reynolds as president of the Royal Academy. Both artists were interested in current events and contributed to the revival of historical painting by taking recent happenings for their subjects. They thus prepared the way for the French painters of the imperial epic, and to this extent were pioneers. In the year VI, General Pommereul, the translator of Milizia, lamented that the "miracles of the Revolution, and the unheard-of prodigies" of the French armies had not yet found "either painters or engravers." He wished art to become a vehicle for education and propaganda, so as to "correct Europe's ideas about a Revolution which has been too much reviled." (See Edgar Wind, "The Revolution of History Painting," *Journal of the Warburg and Courtauld Institutes* 2 [1938–39]:116–27.)

Charles Willson Peale and Gilbert Stuart worked under West in London before becoming portrait painters in the United States. In 1789 Peale executed a portrait of Benjamin Franklin, one of his most characteristic works. (See Charles Coleman Sellers, "Portraits and Miniatures by Charles Willson Peale," *Transactions of the American Philosophical Society*, n.s., pt. 1 [June 1952]:1–369.) The sheet of paper in Franklin's left hand has written on it one of his famous passages on lightning and conductors. Actually, in 1789 Franklin was occupied with black emancipation and signed *An Address to the Public, from the Pennsylvania Society for Promoting the Abolition of Slavery, and the Relief of free Negroes unlawfully held in Bondage.*

ROME AND NEOCLASSICISM

1. In 1789 Prud'hon was already thirty-one years old. He had just returned from Italy, despite Canova's supposed attempts to make him stay. In Italy he had discovered Leonardo, and above all Correggio. In Paris during the early days of the Revolution he was little known, but he flourished under the Consulate and the Empire. His work during the Revolutionary period included both allegories on themes of love and allegories on civic themes. To the first category belong *L'Amour séduit l'Innocence, le Plaisir l'entraîne, le Repentir suit; L'Amour réduit à la raison*; and *L'Union de l'Amour et de l'Amitié.* And to the second: *Le Génie de la Liberté; La Tyrannie;* and *La Constitution française: La Sagesse unit la Loi avec la Liberté et celle-ci appelle à l'union de la Nature avec tous ses droits.* See Jean Guiffrey, *L'Œuvre de Pierre-Paul Prud'hon*, Archives de l'art français, nouvelle période, XIII, 1924.

2. Quatremère de Quincy, *Canova et ses ouvrages* ... (Paris, 1834), p. 17.

3. Joubert, p. 15.

4. Goethe, *Maximen und Reflexionen*, 1113, in *Werke* (Zurich, 1948), 9:639.

5. Louis Hautecoeur, in his thesis *Rome et la renaissance de l'Antiquité à la fin du XVIIIe siècle* (Paris, 1912), devotes a chapter to "radical classicism" and the aesthetic aims of the

artists who practiced line drawing:

"They wanted to attain the most general and permanent kind of Beauty, and so they came to eliminate all that was only accident, including color and even shade. Drawing, which circumscribes form and is thus the most intellectual of the plastic elements, became the only important one, and was reduced to the indicating of contours. Line drawing, which is an abstraction, seemed to them the logical method for depicting their ideas.

"The simplicity of this process had already attracted some engravers: In 1770 Barbault had done line reproductions of antique bas-reliefs and pateras, and Canova had used the same method to reproduce the detail of some bronzes from Herculaneum. The idea soon emerged of using this kind of drawing to teach students 'purity of line.' In 1785 Volpato and Morghen published models of statues '*in simplici contorni con pochi ombre.*' But although in eighteenth-century eyes these statues were devoid of colour, they did still cast shadows; and excavation had made fashionable a whole class of works in which the Ancients had already done as the reformers wished. Were not the Greek vases perfect examples of line drawing?" (p. 243).

6. François Hemsterhuis, *Œuvres philosophiques*, 3 vols., ed. L. S. P. Meyboom (Leuworde, 1846), 1:16–18, 32.

7. According to Hemsterhuis in his *Lettre sur la Sculpture* (1769), calm and majesty in sculpture corresponded to a psychological need for the swiftest possible perception, for a kind of instant apprehension. "Unity or simplicity are therefore one of its necessary principles. But as by nature the beauties of sculpture are seen from all sides and from every possible angle, it tries to and must please from a distance as much as from close to, and perhaps even more. For this reason I believe it should try to minimize as far as possible the time I need to arrive at an idea of the subject, through the ease and excellence of its contours,

rather than maximize the number of ideas involved, through a complete expression of the subject's actions and passions. From this would naturally follow the required calm and majesty."

Hemsterhuis, like Winckelmann, thus opts for the calm beauty of form as against the quest for character. (On the aesthetic problem of godlike calm, see Walter Rehm, *Götterstille und Göttertrauer* [Salzburg, 1951].)

8. Hemsterhuis, p. 35.

9. Carl Ludwig Fernow, *Leben des Künstlers Asmus Jakob Carstens . . .* (Leipzig, 1806).

10. Ibid., p. 254.

The supreme importance of form, drawing, and line—a principle strictly adhered to by the neoclassicists—found one of its clearest formulations in Kant (§ 14 of the *Critique of Judgment*, 1790). Color is a physical attraction and appeals too directly to our senses, whereas line permits a disinterested pleasure: "In painting, sculpture, and in fact in all the formative arts, in architecture and horticulture, so far as fine arts, the *design* is what is essential. Here it is not what gratifies in sensation but merely what pleases by its form, that is the fundamental prerequisite for taste. The colours which give brilliancy to the sketch are part of the charm. They may no doubt, in their own way, enliven the object for sensation, but make it really worth looking at and beautiful they cannot. Indeed, more often than not the requirements of the beautiful form restrict them to a very narrow compass, and, even where charm is admitted, it is only this form that gives them a place of honour" (Immanuel Kant, *The Critique of Judgement*, trans. with analytical indexes by James Creed Meredith [Oxford, Clarendon Press, 1952], §14, p. 67).

Canova and the Absent Gods

1. Quatremère de Quincy, *Canova*, p. 34.

2. Ibid., pp. 34–35.

3. Ibid., p. 33.

4. Rudolf Zeitler, *Klassizismus und Utopia*, Fig. 5 (Stockholm, 1954), p. 97.

5. Quatremère de Quincy, *Canova*, p. 49.

6. Friederike Brun, *Römische Tagebuch*, in *Prosaische Schriften* (Zürich, 1800), p. 208, quoted from Zeitler, p. 208.

7. Zeitler, p. 102.

8. "One day [in 1788] when I [Mme Vigée-Lebrun] had invited a dozen or fifteen people to come that evening and hear a reading by the poet Lebrun, my brother, during my rest, read me a few pages from the *Travels of Anarcharsis*. When he came to the passage which describes a Greek dinner and explains how to make some of the sauces, he said, 'We ought to serve this to our guests tonight.' I at once sent for my cook and told her what I had in mind; and we agreed on her making one kind of sauce for the chicken and another for the eel. As I was expecting some very pretty women, I thought we would all dress up in Greek costume so as to give a surprise to M. de Vaudreuil and M. Boutin, who weren't to arrive until ten o'clock. I could get all the clothes I needed from my studio, which was full of stuff I used to drape my models, and the comte de Parois, who lived in my house in the rue de Cléry, had a superb collection of Etruscan vases. He came to see me that day at about four o'clock, I told him of my plan, and he brought me a lot of goblets and vases for me to choose from. I cleaned them all myself and arranged them on a mahogany table without a cloth. Then I put a big screen

behind the chairs and covered it with a large drapery looped up at intervals as in the paintings of Poussin. A hanging lamp shed a bright light on the table. All was ready, including my costumes, when the first guest arrived, the charming Mme Chalgrin, daughter of Joseph Vernet. Then came Mme de Bonneuil, noted for her beauty; then Mme Vigée, my sister-in-law, who though not pretty had the most beautiful eyes. All three ladies were metamorphosed into real Athenians. Then Lebrun Pindar came, and we took off his powder and combed his side-curls straight and I put a laurel crown on his head. . . . The comte de Parois happened to have a big crimson cloak which I could use to drape my poet, whom in the twinkling of an eye I turned into both Pindar and Anacreon. Then came the marquis de Cubières. While we sent to his place for a guitar he had had adapted into a golden lyre, I dressed him up.

"It was getting late. I didn't have much time to think about myself, but as I always wore white gowns in the form of a tunic, nowadays called smocks, all I needed was a veil and a wreath of flowers on my head. I spent most time on my daughter, a sweet child, and on Mlle de Bonneuil, beautiful as an angel. Both looked delightful carrying light antique jars ready to serve us with wine.

"At half-past nine the preparations were complete, and when we all took our places the effect of the table was so novel and picturesque that each of us stood up in turn to look at the others sitting round.

"At ten we heard the carriage of the comte de Vaudreuil and M. Boutin drive in, and when they got to the dining-room door, which I had had set wide open, they found us singing Gluck's chorus *Le Dieu de Paphos et de Gnide*, accompanied by M. de Cubières on the lyre" (*Souvenirs*, 1:67–70).

Mme Vigée-Lebrun presented her Greek supper party as an improvisation in order to make it seem an inexpensive whim: She spent only fifteen francs on it, whereas according to legend it cost tens of thousands. The theme was the revival of the Greek past. We know that Mme de Genlis and David used to organize tableaux vivants at the house of the duc d'Orléans. When we also remember that David's *Oath of the Horatii* was probably inspired by a ballet-pantomime by Noverre, we discover a strange interaction between life, theater, painting, and a nostalgic image of Antiquity, the latter exerting an intense fascination precisely because it was far away. (See Edgar Wind, "The Sources of David's *Horaces*," *Journal of the Warburg and Courtauld Institutes* 4 [1940–41]:124–38.) David's *Horatii* itself inspired an opera, with libretto by Guillard and music by Salieri, Gluck's favorite pupil. According to Wind, the *Paris and Helen* exhibited in the 1789 Salon might have been influenced by Gluck's opera *Paride ed Elena*.

9. People's historical consciousness grew keener in the last part of the eighteenth century. It is worth noting that L. Lanzi's *Storia Pittorica dell'Italia* was published in 1789 and Herder's *Ideen* between 1784 and 1791.

In France, even at the time of revolutionary iconoclasm, masterpieces and other records of the past began to be preserved more systematically. The Republican government took over a project from the Ancien Régime, and the *grande galerie* of the Louvre was to become a "Museum" housing the pictures of the old royal collections. Alexandre Lenoir organized a Musée des Monuments français at the convent des Petits-Augustins, where he assembled the most important remains of churches and chateaux that had been destroyed. There was also an "Elysée" bristling with "constructions" as in landscape gardens. Lenoir wanted to link the architectural survivals with the remains of great men, to create a place where knowledge of the past, admiration for national glory, meditation on death, and feeling for nature might all merge together. Lenoir's project shows how two typical revolutionary institutions, the museum and the pantheon, both derived from one desire—the desire to combine knowledge of history with homage to exemplary great men. Soufflot's church of Sainte-Geneviève, with alterations by Quatremère de Quincy, became the center of a civic cult: It was a common mausoleum of the dead, those in whom the collective consciousness chose to see itself reflected. It might be called a museum of great names and great lives.

10. It was as if the period itself was trying to balance the frivolous grace of a sculptor like Clodion with the gloomy sentimentality of those like Banks, Flaxman, and Schadow. Sergel, going from the Dionysiac "demonism" of his *Faune ivre* to the cold meditativeness of his huge *Anges*, expresses this oscillation in his own particular way. But between these two contrasting tendencies there emerged with some difficulty an art at once discreet, flexible, and strong, in which concern with reality did not preclude an aura of mystery, in which the present moment of the portrait seemed to hold a secret element of time: I refer to Houdon. The bust of his daughter Sabine is a true labor of love. The Revolution was not kind to Houdon, and after 1789, when he executed portraits of Bailly, La Fayette, and Mirabeau, he devoted himself increasingly to teaching.

There grew up, in a somewhat feverish fashion, a statuary of emblems and symbols. The sculptors concerned were Chinard, Michallon, Moitte, Roland, Beauvallet, Lesueur, Corbet, Espercieux, Ramey, Chaudet, and Cartellier, who were indebted both to their great precedessors Pigalle and Pajou and to the antique models and encouragement of David. Schadow, in Prussia, abandoning Winckelmann's precepts and soon in conflict with Goethe, tried to reconcile classical grace and dignity with exact imitation. His "realism," like that of Houdon, managed to combine a somewhat disturbing individuality with an element from the realm of pure form.

The Reconciliation with Darkness

1. Goethe, *Beiträge zur Optik* (Weimar, 1791; rpt. Olms, 1964), p. 15, §24.

2. See also Goethe, *Entwurf einer Farbenlehre*, Einleitung, in *Sämtliche Werke*, 6 vols. (Cotta, 1863), 6:136.

3. "Goethe derived his circle of colors from duality. He distinguishes the circle's positive side, which is near the light (yellow to red) from the negative side (blue to violet), which borders on darkness. In the first group of colors we find the "exploits of light," and in the others its "sufferings" (Marianne Trapp, *Goethes naturphilosophische Denkweise* [Stuttgart, 1949], p. 75).

4. Goethe, *Faust I*, Studierzimmer, *Sämtliche Werke*, Jubiläumsausgabe, vol. 13, p. 55.

Goya

1. Because he knew how to accept the dark, Goya's art was the only one of its time that succeeded in making light and its infinite modulations the very stuff of painting. In all other work, especially that of artists who bowed to the tyranny of line, *lighting* was superadded to form. At the end of a meticulous study of color in the work of Goya, Jutta Held writes: "From David on, the French increasingly related color and light to separate objects. In Goya, on the other hand, light and darkness and the various color values (which ultimately include light and shade), remain elements in themselves, less subordinated to the requirements of representation" (*Farbe und Licht in Goyas Malerei* [Ber-

lin, 1964], p. 159). Goya's painting thus foreshadows the audacities of Manet.

2. My comparison of the most violent of Goya's later works and the arguments in the *Critique of Judgment* (1790) may have caused some surprise.

Let us remind ourselves that Kant, like Burke, suggested a dual aesthetic: that of beauty and that of the sublime. The beautiful was defined as that which pleases "quite disinterestedly," "universally and without concept"; it was "the form of the *finality* of an object in so far as it is perceived in that object without its end being represented"; beauty is recognized "without concept as the object of a necessary satisfaction." Genius is sole master of the free play of imagination, and of imagination's relation with the laws of understanding; precepts are vain here, for nature alone, through genius, dictates the laws of art. This aesthetic of the beautiful legitimized the soaring development of decoration, which at the end of the eighteenth century attained the most exquisite delicacy of touch and complete mastery of its own language.

The aesthetic of the sublime, on the other hand, is concerned with a kind of thought which, at the formidable sight of external reality, becomes aware of the radical difference which makes man essentially invulnerable to the crushing powers of nature: "The sublime is that, the mere capacity of thinking of which evidences a faculty of mind transcending every standard of sense" (§25, Meredith trans., p. 98).

"True sublimity must be sought only in the mind of the judging Subject, and not in the Object of nature that occasions this attitude by the estimate formed of it. Who would apply the term 'sublime' even to shapeless mountain masses towering one above the other in wild disorder with their pyramids of ice, or to the dark tempestuous ocean, and such like things? But in the contemplation of them, without any regard to their form, the mind abandons itself to the imagination and to a reason placed, though quite apart from any definite end, in conjunction therewith, and merely broadening its view, it feels itself elevated in its own estimate of itself on finding all the might of the imagination still unequal to its ideas"(§26, pp. 104–5).

"Therefore the feeling of the sublime in nature is respect for our own vocation, which we attribute to the Object of nature by a certain subreption (substitution of a respect for the Object in place of one for the idea of humanity in our own self—the Subject); and this feeling renders, as it were, intuitable the supremacy of our cognitive faculties on the rational side over the greatest faculty of sensibility" (§27, p. 106).

"Bold, overhanging, and, as it were, threatening rocks, thunderclouds piled up in the vault of heaven, borne along with flashes and peals, volcanoes in all their violence of destruction, hurricanes leaving desolation in their track, the boundless ocean rising with rebellious force, the high waterfall of some mighty river, and the like, make our power of resistance of trifling moment in comparison with their might. But, provided our own position is secure, their aspect is all the more attractive for its fearfulness; and we readily call these objects sublime, because they raise the forces of the soul above the height of vulgar commonplace, and discover within us a power of resistance of quite another kind, which gives us courage to be able to measure ourselves against the seeming omnipotence of nature" (§28, pp. 110–11).

"Sublimity, therefore, does not reside in any of the things of nature, but only in our own mind, in so far as we may become conscious of our superiority over nature within, and thus also over nature without us (as exerting influence upon us). Everything which provokes this feeling in us, including the *might* of nature which challenges our strength, is then, though improperly, called sublime, and it is only under presupposition of this idea within us, and in relation to it, that we are capable of attaining to the idea of the sublimity of that Being which inspires deep respect in us, not merely by the display of its might in nature, but more by the faculty which is planted in us of estimating that might without fear, and of regarding our estate as exalted above it" (§28, p. 114).

Kant's aesthetic of the sublime applies first and foremost to works like the storms of Joseph Vernet and the Alps of Caspar Wolf or Ludwig Hess. It presupposes in the spectator a sense of security which seems unable to survive in the world of Goya, profoundly as he may have been attached, as Hubert Damisch rightly says, to "divine reason" ("L'Art de Goya et les contradictions de l'esprit des Lumières," in *Utopie et Institutions au XVIIIᵉ siècle* [Paris, The Hague, 1963]). We may wonder if Goya, who no longer depicted the attractive horrors of nature but instead the horrors of war (an expression of "the radical evil in man"), still left open the subjective dimension in which Kant's "feeling of superiority" existed. Theodor Hetzer, speaking of the *Disasters of War*, wrote: "Nothing distracts us or diverts our attention. Nothing offers us reconciliation. For nothing leads us to a general order, nothing suggests a law which might assure us of a solid earth and persuade us to believe that even in the horrible there is a necessity of fate, a will of God. Intensification through art does not lead to deliverance; it increases our feeling of oppression, our nightmare. In the last works of Rembrandt, Titian, and Velasquez, art leads from the concrete to a transfiguration; but Goya's art leads to something spectral. The great artist's path always diverges from the multiplicity and the nearness of things in order to attain to the visionary state. But the visions of Goya are not lit by eternal light; they are darkness, and the void behind it" (*Aufsätze und Vorträge*, 2 vols. [Leipzig, 1957], vol. 1, *Francisco Goya und die Krise der Kunst um 1800*, p. 196). Yes, the harmony of the universe has disappeared over the earthly horizon. We have no reassurance now, no consolation; heaven is closed. But art, and the mind's opposition to the fascination of horror, only take on the more importance. If the human universe eludes our efforts to understand, our only resource is denunciation. Clearly, beyond a certain point, the art of Goya can no longer be measured in terms of the Kantian idea of the sublime, not because the consciousness of the spectator is not called on to feel the superiority of all consciousness over that which crushes man, but because deep down the universe of Goya no longer suggests the presence of a meaning. The same experience of absurd horror is expressed in the famous passage in the *Mémoires d'outre-tombe*, where Chateaubriand, from his hotel window, sees rioters brandishing the decapitated heads of Foulon and Berthier toward him on the ends of their pikes. As Eric Weil has shown (in *Problèmes kantiens* [Paris, 1963]), the *Critique of Judgment* tries to make us admit that "natural and historical reality *is*, and is *meaningful*, because everything is a meaningful Whole"; in short, that meaning and fact, far from being opposed to one another, are the same. Goya seems to have been haunted by the opposite belief. But he did not paint in order to impart that conviction, but rather to try to exorcise and cure himself of it.

3. During the eighteenth century, new techniques in color engraving and the use of aquatint and mezzotint led to the widespread diffusion of "picturesque views," as well as of pictures of sentimental anecdote, scenes of gallantry, and political satire. The 1770s and 1780s reflected a great curiosity about the mountains, and there were many examples of "travels in the Alps." While, following the lead given by Shaftesbury and Rousseau, fine texts were written describing waterfalls, rocks, and mountain peaks (e.g., Ramond de Carbonnières, Bourrit, De Luc, and above all Horace-Bénédict de Saussure, whose *Voyages dans les Alpes* was a European success in 1787), at the same time countless engravings were being published. It was a minor, documentary genre, and the artists concerned often remained obscure. Around 1780 Caspar Wolf painted fairylike mountain scenes for a Berne dealer who had them engraved and sold

widely throughout the rest of the century.

Watercolor, an intimate and extraordinarily flexible genre, flourished particularly in England, with Paul Sandby, Alexander Cozens, his son John Robert, and Francis Towne—all precursors of Girtin, Constable, and Turner. The watercolor artist felt all the more free because landscape from nature was regarded as an inferior art. The academic salons of Paris and London usually accepted only "composite landscapes"—epic or idyllic landscapes in which the painter rearranged and recomposed in his studio (transforming "rough" nature into "beautiful" nature) the various elements he had taken from the life. The watercolorist, though less highly esteemed, was more master of his art. Winckelmann had incautiously said that landscape did not greatly concern the soul: "The pleasures in general, even those which cost man time, his most precious possession, only delight and interest him insofar as they to a greater or lesser degree attract his mind. Purely material sensations merely brush against the soul, leaving no lasting trace: Such is the pleasure given us by the sight of a landscape picture or still life. In order to judge such works we need make no greater mental effort than the artist used to paint them; the mere connoisseur of even layman may consider himself exempt from taking any trouble." (*Various Collected Pieces on the Arts*.)

True, the feeling for pastoral was dying out in England. It was losing strength in France (despite the continuing vogue for Gessner, and Delille's translation of the *Georgics*). In Germany and Austria it lingered on a little (Haydn only finished *The Seasons* in 1801, and Beethoven's *Pastoral Symphony* dates from 1808). It was no longer so easy to believe in the poetic fiction of rural happiness. A myth was fading: The peasantry did not live in the golden age, as Crabbe's fine poem *The Village* (1783) bitterly observes. Not only did the soot of industry contaminate the countryside, but rural hardship overflowed to swell the numbers of the urban industrial proletariat.

It was hard for "composite landscapes" to take rural idyll as their subject. But the past still remained: the image of the legendary Arcadia, of the Sicily of Theocritus, or some tropical mirage inspired by Bougainville's *Voyage* or by Bernardin de Saint-Pierre's *Paul et Virginie* (1787). A few painters, among them some northern ones like Tischbein and Koch, were attracted by the light of Italy and the idea of ideal harmony and tried in vain to rediscover the secret of Poussin. But here too disillusion prevailed. In the complex tragedy *Torquato Tasso*, completed in 1789, Goethe's underlying criticism corrodes the beliefs of his characters; for Goethe can believe neither in the Arcadian golden age of memory in which his solitary hero seeks refuge nor in the communion of noble souls, Princess Leonora d'Este's interiorized substitute for the world's early happiness. The poet has no right to escape from the world that surrounds him.

Félix Nogaret, a civic poet of the French Revolution (one of the "Tyrtaei"), expressed the same belief more crudely in a hymn significantly called *Le Procès de l'Age d'or* (The Golden Age on Trial). With the aid of some ponderous periphrasis, Nogaret lauds the age of warlike metallurgy:

"Advocates of the golden age and the age of Rhea,
Be silent. . . . I have sworn to destroy your altars.
Forge spears, serve the republic:
Make haste . . . we love the harmonies of hammers.
It was iron and steel that protected the cradle
And created the treasures of the Swiss nation.
> Thence flew the shaft that pierced
> The breast of the bloodthirsty monster.
> Without lead, iron and bronze,
> There is no liberty on earth."

In France the work of Louis Moreau the Elder (1739–1805) advanced cautiously towards real landscape, capturing its inflections and lighting with moving sobriety and without recourse to "interesting" anecdote. It had something in common, including certain dreamy contemplations of sky and cloud, with the spirit of the English watercolorists (though it did not venture on the seashore or on Alpine precipices). P. H. Valenciennes, who was some eleven years older than Louis Moreau, did many sketches from life in the Roman Campagna. He was an observer of the physical atmosphere, and his *Eléments de perspective pratique* (an VIII) contains astonishingly pertinent remarks about accidental light, shadow, the different times of day, clouds, storms, and volcanic eruptions. But Valenciennes was too attached to the ideal of the "composite landscape" to attribute any independent value to his works done from life: He regarded them as no more than preparatory exercises. He painted his *ressouvenirs* or remembrances in his studio, as Corot was still to do later.

Valencienne's *Eléments* shows two complementary tendencies which were to be characteristic of romanticism, or at least of some of its fundamental leanings. The first tendency notes the disappearance or destruction by time of the legendary sites of pastoral happiness:

"What has become of the fragrant woods of Paphos and Amathonte? What has become of that happy Arcadia which the poets vied each other in praising? What remains of the delightful valley of Tempe, sheltered by Mounts Olympus and Pierus, watered by the river Peneus, and covered with forests dense and ever green? The mountains, rivers, and valleys still exist, but they are no longer what they were. The soil may still be fertile, but the crops it grows are different. Instead of the peaceful inhabitants who once sang of their happiness and wellbeing, miserable slaves are sunk in ignorance and want. And going through these famous regions, the traveler is surprised to feel no other pleasure than the memory of their ancient splendor. True, the imagination can transport us back to the time of their glory; one seems to see all they have lost; one questions the rocks, sole

[281]

remaining witnesses of past grandeur. The silent valleys, the barren plains, the stagnant waters all inspire pity and regret. In vain one tries to think of these delightful places decked in all Nature can offer of smiling variety; the eyes see only a gaunt skeleton scarcely suggesting what it was in its brilliant youth."

But instead of looking to art for a melancholy representation of these ruins and this return to the wilderness, Valenciennes hopes that the imagination, guided by literary sensibility and archaeological erudition, will endeavor to reconstruct both the physical appearance of the past and its poetic aspect. Painting is given the task of bringing about a resurrection that will not only conjure up a mental landscape from the canvas but also reconstruct ruined cities in terms of what they truly were in the past.

"Since the artist no longer finds, on the actual site, Nature such as he conceived it in his imagination, he must recreate it in accordance with the descriptions of the poets who have depicted it with the most grandeur and elegance. Thus, familiar with the Nature that is daily before his eyes, and identifying himself, through his reading, with the Nature that is only ideal, he can, if he combines them with taste, lend them a new style, new forms, brighter colors, and consequently a physiognomy to match" (pp. 484–85). "A Ruin which shows us only the remains of an artificial object which once existed in its entirety gives us but the cold and depressing skeleton of a more or less dilapidated building. . . . A sensitive and philosophical artist will prefer to paint the monuments of Greece and Rome as they were in the days of their splendor" (pp. 413–14).

We are here as far away as possible from that direct contemplation of the world which at the end of the eighteenth century now had the necessary technical means at its disposal. For the art of landscape to develop fully, an end had to be made of the classical distinction between "nature as it is" and "nature as it might be." Artists needed to renounce the idea of a perfected Nature which hovered in the margin of the great poems of antiquity. But that did not mean they had to renounce the idea of perfection: It was enough to proclaim that perfection is present, and paradise revealed, in the nature immediately before us— if only the artist has learned to look at the world searchingly enough to make out the inner laws of what he sees.

LIGHT AND POWER IN *The Magic Flute*

1. See Siegfried Morenz, *Die Zauberflöte* (Münster-Cologne, 1952); J. and B. Massin, *Mozart* (Paris, 1959); A. Rosenberg, *Die Zauberflöte* (Munich, 1964); J. Chailley, *La Flûte enchantée, opéra maçonnique* (Paris, 1968).

2. According to Chailley (p. 135), the swoon symbolizes the dying to the self that precedes initiation ordeals.

3. The priests' words begin the presto of the finale of act 1. All subsequent references are by act and scene numbers and appear in text.

4. Reinhart Koselleck, *Kritik und Krise* (Frankfurt, 1966).

5. This is Jacques Chailley's theory.

6. All commentators were to stress this point, especially Chailley.

7. *Rapport relatif aux personnes incarcérées*, 8 Ventose, an 2.

8. Goethe, *Sämtliche Werke*, Jubiläumsausgabe, vol. 8, *Singspiele*, pp. 310–11.
On Goethe's singspiels see Hugo von Hofmannsthal's admirable study in *Gesammelte Werke, Prosa IV* (S. Fischer, 1955), pp. 174–81.

Short Bibliography

1

Some Sources

Some further reading is suggested in the following list of works on the theory of aesthetics. The list does not include all the books quoted in the body of the text. Goethe, Schiller, Kant, André Chénier, Burke, Blake, and so on are of the first importance, but I shall confine my suggestions to authors less well known and less frequently read.

Boullée, E. L. *Architecture: Essai sur l'art.* Textes réunis et présentés par J. M. Pérouse de Montclos. Paris, 1968.

Fernow, C. L. *Römische Studien.* 3 vols. Zürich, 1803.

――*Leben des Künstlers Asmus Jacob Carstens.* Leipzig, 1806.

Fuseli. *The Mind of Henry Fuseli, Selections from his Writings.* Introduction by Eudo C. Mason. London, 1951.

Guiffrey, J. *Collection des livrets des anciens Salons de peinture depuis 1673 jusqu'en 1800.* 42 vols. Paris, 1869–1872.

――*Table générale des artistes ayant exposé aux Salons du XVIIIᵉ siècle, suivie d'une table de la bibliographie des Salons.* Paris, 1873.

Hemsterhuis, F. *Œuvres philosophiques*. New ed. 2 vols. Paris, 1809.

Ledoux, C.-N. *L'Architecture considérée sous le rapport de l'art, des moeurs et de la législation*. 1804. Facsimile ed. Paris, 1962.

Lenoir, A. *Observations scientifiques et critiques sur le génie*. Paris, 1821.

Mengs, A. R. *Opere*. 2 vols. Parma, 1780.

——*Œuvres Complètes*. Paris, 1786.

Milizia, F. *Dell'arte di vedere nelle belle arti*. Venice, 1781.

Moritz, K. Ph. *Ueber die bildende Nachahmung des Schönen*. Brunswick, 1788.

Preciado de la Vega, F. *Arcadia Pictórica en sueño ó poema pro-saico sobre la Teórica y Práctica de la Pintura*. Madrid, 1789.

Quatremère de Quincy, A. C. *Dissertation sur les opéras bouffons italiens*. N.p., 1789.

——*Considérations sur les arts du dessin en France, suivies d'un plan d'Académie*. Paris, 1791.

——*Encyclopédie méthodique: Architecture*. 3 vols. Paris, 1788–1825.

——*Canova et ses ouvrages*. Paris, 1834.

Reynolds, Sir J. *Discourses* . . . London, 1769–91.

Valenciennes, P. H. *Eléments de perspective pratique*. Paris, an VIII.

Winckelmann, J. J. *Sämtliche Werke*. 8 vols. Donaueschingen, 1825–1835.

2

IMPORTANT STUDIES OF THE PERIOD

Adhémar, J. *La Gravure originale au XVIIIe siècle*. Paris, 1963.

Aulard, A. *Le Culte de la Raison et le culte de l'Etre suprême (1793–1794)*. Paris, 1909.

Baczko, B. *Lumières de l'utopie*. Paris, 1978.

Baltrusaitis, J. *La Quête d'Isis*. Paris, 1967.

Benoît, F. *L'Art français sous la Révolution et l'Empire: Les doctrines, les idées, les genres*. Paris, 1897.

Blondel, S. *L'Art pendant la Révolution*. Paris, n.d.

Cassirer, E. *Freiheit und Form*. 3d ed. Darmstadt, 1961.

———*Die Philosophie der Aufklärung*. Tübingen, 1932.

De David à Delacroix: La peinture française de 1774 à 1830. Catalogue of the Exhibition Held at the Grand Palais in Paris, 1974. Bibliography.

Despois, E. *Le Vandalisme révolutionnaire; fondations littéraires, scientifiques et artistiques de la Convention*. Paris, 1868.

Friedlander, W. *David to Delacroix*. Tr. R. Goldwater. Harvard, 1952.

Furet, F. *Penser la Révolution française*. Paris, 1978.

———, and Richet, D. *La Révolution*. 2 vols. Paris, 1965–66.

Gautier, H. *L'an 1789*. Paris, 1888.

Godechot, J. *La Prise de la Bastille*. Paris, 1965. Bibliography.

Goncourt, E., and J. de. *Histoire de la société française pendant la Révolution*. Paris, 1854.

Grigson, G. *The Harp of Aeolus*. London, 1947.

Hautecoeur, L. *Rome et la renaissance de l'antiquité à la fin du XVIIIe siècle*. Paris, 1912.

————*Littérature et peinture en France du XVIIe au XXe siècle*. Paris, 1942.

————*L'Art sous la Révolution et l'Empire, 1789–1815*. Paris, 1953.

Hawley, H. *Neo-classicism, Style and Motif*. Cleveland Museum of Art. New York, 1964.

Honour, H. *Neo-classicism*. Harmondsworth, 1968.

Johnson, J. W. *The Formation of English Neoclassical Thought*. Princeton, N.J., 1966.

Lankheit, K. *Revolution und Restauration*. Baden-Baden, 1965. Bibliography.

Leith, J. A. *The Idea of Art as Propaganda in France, 1750–1799*. Toronto, 1965.

Lemaître, H. *Le Paysage anglais à l'aquarelle*. Paris, 1955.

Leymarie, J. *La Peinture française: Le dix-neuvième siècle*. Geneva, 1962. Bibliography.

Michelet, J. *Histoire de la Révolution française*. 7 vols. Paris, 1847–53.

Monglond, A. *Histoire intérieure du préromantisme français*. 2 vols. 1929. New ed. Paris, 1965–66.

Ozouf, M. *La Fête révolutionnaire, 1789–1799*. Paris, 1976.

Pariset, F. G. "Le néo-classicisme." *L'Information d'histoire de l'art*, Paris, March-April 1959.

Praz, M. *Gusto neoclassico*. 2d ed. Naples, 1959.

Rehm, W. *Griechentum und Goethezeit: Geschichte eines Glaubens*. Leipzig, 1936.

———*Götterstille und Göttertrauer*. Salzburg, 1951.

Renouvier, J. *Histoire de l'art pendant la Révolution, considéré principalement dans les estampes*. Paris, 1863.

Rosenblum, R. *Transformations in Late Eighteenth Century Art*. Princeton, N.J., 1967.

Scheffler, H. *Das Phänomen der Kunst: Grundsätzliche Betrachtungen zum 19. Jahrhundert*. Munich, 1952.

Starobinski, J. *L'Invention de la liberté*. Geneva, 1964.

Tocqueville, A. de. *L'Ancien Régime et la Révolution*. Œuvres complètes, bk. 2. 2 vols. Paris, 1952.

Trahard, P. *La Sensibilité révolutionnaire*. Paris, 1936.

Viatte, A. *Les Sources occultes du romantisme, 1770–1820*. 2 vols. Paris, 1928.

Zeitler, R. *Klassizismus und Utopia: Interpretationen zu Werken von David, Canova, Carstens, Thorvaldsen, Koch*. Stockholm, 1954. Bibliography.

3

MONOGRAPHS

BLAKE

Frye, N. *Fearful Symmetry: A Study of William Blake*. Princeton, N.J., 1947.

Keynes, G. *William Blake's Engravings*. London, 1950.

BOILLY

Marmottan, P. *Le Peintre Louis Boilly (1761–1845)*. Paris, 1913.

CANOVA

Bassi, E. *La Gipsoteca di Possagno: Sculture e dipinta di Canova*. Venice, 1957.

CHINARD

Rocher-Jauneau, M. "Chinard and the Empire Style." *Apollo* 80, no. 31 (1964):220–25.

DAVID

Adhémar, J., and Cassou, J. *David: Naissance du génie d'un peintre*. Paris, 1953.

Dowd, D. L. *Pageant Master of the Republic: Jacques-Louis David and the French Revolution*. Lincoln, Neb., 1948.

Hautecoeur, L. *Louis David*. Paris, 1954.

Holma, K. *David, son évolution et son style*. Paris, 1940.

Wilhelm, J. "David et ses portraits." *Art de France* no. 4 (1964):158–73.

DESPREZ

Wollin, N. G. *Gravures originales de Desprez.* Malmö, 1933.
———*Desprez en Italie.* Malmö, 1934.
———*Desprez en Suède.* Stockholm, 1939.

FUSELI

Henry Fuseli. Catalogue of the Exhibition Held at the Tate Gallery, London, in 1975.
Schiff, G. *Zeichnungen von Johann-Heinrich Füssli.* Zürich, 1959.
———*Johann-Heinrich Füssli.* Catalogue raisonné. 2 vols. Zürich, 1973.

GONZAGA

Muraro, M. T., *Scenografie di Pietro Gonzaga.* Catalogue of the Exhibition Held in Venice in 1967.

GOYA

Damisch, H. "L'Art de Goya et les contradictions de l'esprit des Lumières." *Utopie et institutions au XVIIIᵉ siècle.* Ed. P. Francastel. The Hague, 1963.
Desparmet Fitz-Gerald, X. *L'Œuvre peint de Goya.* 4 vols. Paris, 1928–50.
Du Gué Trapier, E. *Goya and his Sitters: A study of His Style as a Portraitist.* New York, 1964.
Gassier, P., and Wilson, J. *Œuvre et vie de Francisco Goya.* Freiburg, 1970.
Gudiol, J. *Goya.* 4 vols. Barcelona-Paris, 1971.
Held, J. *Farbe und Licht in Goyas Malerei.* Berlin, 1964. Bibliography.
Helman, E. *Trasmundo de Goya.* Madrid, 1963.
Hetzer, Th. "Francisco Goya und die Krise der Kunst um 1800." In *Aufsätze und Vorträge.* 2 vols. Leipzig, 1957.
Lafuente Ferrari, E. *Goya.* Paris, 1950.

Malraux, A. *Saturne: Essai sur Goya*. Paris, 1950.

Nordström, F. *Goya, Saturn and Melancholy*. Stockholm, 1962. Bibliography and Chronological Table.

Sambricio, V. de. *Tapices de Goya*. Madrid, 1946.

Sanchez Canton, F. J. *Goya*. Paris, 1930.

Goya and His Times. Catalogue of the Winter Exhibition Held at the Royal Academy of Arts, London, 1963–64. Bibliography.

GREUZE

Martin, J. *L'Œuvre de J.-B. Greuze*. Catalogue raisonné. Paris, 1908.

GUARDI

Byam Shaw, J. *The Drawings of Francesco Guardi*. London, 1951.

Fiocco, G. *Guardi*. Milan, Silvana, 1965. Bibliography.

Problemi guardeschi. Atti del convegno di studi promosso dalla mostra dei Guardi, Venice, 13–14 September 1965. Published in Venice 1967.

Zampetti, P. *Mostra dei Guardi*. Catalogue of the Exhibition Held in Venice in 1965. Bibliography.

HOUDON

Réau, L. *Houdon, sa vie et son œuvre*. 2 vols. Paris, 1964.

PRUD'HON

Guiffrey, J. *L'Œuvre de Pierre-Paul Prud'hon*. Archives de l'art français, novelle période, XIII, 1924.

QUARENGHI

Disegni di Giacomo Quarenghi. Catalogue of the Exhibition Held in Venice, 1967. Introduction by Giuseppe Fiocco. Bibliography.

ROBERT

Montgolfier, B. de. "Hubert Robert, peintre de Paris au musée Carnavalet." *Bulletin du musée Carnavalet*, 1964, année 17, 1–2, pp. 2–35.

TIEPOLO

Byam Shaw, J. *The Drawings of Domenico Tiepolo*. London, 1962.

VIGÉE-LEBRUN

Hautecoeur, L. *Madame Vigée-Lebrun*. Paris, 1926.

4

ARCHITECTURE

Guillerme, J. "Lequeu et l'invention du mauvais goût." *Gazette des Beaux-Arts*, 1965, année 107, période 6, bk. 66, pt. 1160, pp. 153–66.

Hautecoeur, L. *L'Architecture classique à Saint-Pétersbourg à la fin du XVIIIe siècle*. Paris, 1912.

———*Histoire de l'architecture classique en France*. 7 bks. in 9 vols. Paris, 1943–57. New ed. forthcoming. Bks. 4 and 5 to date.

Kaufmann, E. "Three Revolutionary Architects: Boullée, Ledoux, and Lequeu." *Transactions of the American Philosophical Society*, n.s. 51, pt. 3 (1952):431–564.

———*Architecture in the Age of Reason*. Harvard, 1955.

Lemagny, J. C. *Les Architectes visionnaires de la fin du XVIIIe siècle*. Catalogue of the Exhibition Held at the Cabinet des Estampes, Geneva, November 1965-January 1966.

Metken, G. "Jean-Jacques Lequeu ou l'Architecture rêvée." *Gazette des Beaux-Arts*. année 106, période 6, bk. 65, pt. 1155, pp. 213–30.

Pérouse de Montclos, J. M. *Etienne-Louis Boullée (1728–1799): De l'Architecture classique à l'architecture révolutionnaire*. Paris, 1969.

Rosenau, H. *Boullée's Treatise on Architecture*. London, 1953.

———"Boullée and Ledoux as Town-Planners: A Reassessment." *Gazette des Beaux-Arts*, 1964, année 106, période 6, bk. 63, pt. 1142, pp. 172–90.

Summerson, J. *Architecture in Britain: 1530–1830*. Harmondsworth, 1954.

Vogt, A.-M. *Boullées Newton-Denkmal*. Basle, 1969.

———*Russische und französische Revolutions-Architektur, 1917–1789*, Cologne, 1974.

Index of Names

INDEX OF NAMES

List $29.50
paperbk. 14.95